"Out of both biblical conviction and years of experience ... seriously about discipleship, evangelisr ... compassion. Their strength is evident, t... their joy in the gospel intoxicating, their a... viding a lodestar to their lives and service. ... foster "Word-filled women's ministry," m... by men. I hope that some of those men ... ...ors who in consequence reflect on what they can do encourage such ministry in their own churches."

D. A. Carson, Research Professor of New Testament, Trinity Evangelical Divinity School

"Women's ministry is ultimately not about women. Nor is it about programs. It's about the glory of God and the health of his church. *Word-Filled Women's Ministry* is a much-needed resource for both men and women to consider the necessity of ministry among women as well as the centrality of the Word for cultivating a church in which women flourish."

Melissa B. Kruger, Women's Ministry Coordinator, Uptown Church; author, *The Envy of Eve*

"There is no question that the women in your churches will be discipled. The only question is whether they will be discipled by the world or the Word. That's why I'm so excited about *Word-Filled Women's Ministry.* It's more than a book. These contributors represent a movement of teachers guiding women to find hope and freedom and salvation in the gospel of Jesus Christ as revealed in his Word. I couldn't more highly esteem these writers, and I pray that you will take up their charge to take up the Word."

Collin Hansen, Editorial Director, The Gospel Coalition; author, *Blind Spots*

"Here is a book that focuses on the possibilities and not just the problems of ministry among women. It is written by women from a wide range of ministry contexts, but all with hearts that beat with a common gospel rhythm. Every chapter is grounded in Scripture and wonderfully practical. Women and men of the Word, read it and be encouraged by all the gospel possibilities."

Jenny Salt, Dean of Students, Sydney Missionary and Bible College

"A marvelous resource for thoughtful Christians, male and female, who long to see the power of the gospel unleashed in their own lives, in the church, and throughout world."

Colin Smith, Senior Pastor, The Orchard, Arlington Heights, Illinois

"This is a significant subject that I have long been interested in, and the voices of my sisters in this book are as edifying as they are encouraging. Pastors, teachers, elders, and women's ministry leaders alike will benefit from this Bible-based, gospel-centered, local church–focused work. I so resonate with their central thesis—"Profitable ministry among women is grounded in God's Word, grows in the context of God's people, and aims for the glory of Christ"—that I anticipate with joy the flourishing of this vision in the churches."

J. Ligon Duncan III, Chancellor and CEO, Reformed Theological Seminary, Jackson, Mississippi

"*Word-Filled Women's Ministry* is written for the bustling daughters of Christ, who need God's Word to train and sustain them in their various labors. It acknowledges the vast diversity of women's ministries in different churches while calling them to a unified commitment to God's Word. Women grow best as they learn from Scripture, first as it is preached to the gathered church and then as it is explored and explained in the company of other godly women. This book is an incentive to the latter, casting a vision for what can and ought to happen when the Bible takes its rightful place at the center of women's ministry."

Megan Hill, pastor's wife; blogger, *Sunday Women*

"Full of careful biblical teaching and many helpful applications, this book is an invaluable aid for all Christian women to think through their own ministry possibilities. But it is also a highly useful tool for pastors and elders to understand and then activate much-needed biblical opportunities for every ministry in the local church. I hope it will be on the must-read list of every church leader."

David Jackman, Former President, Proclamation Trust, London, England

"Gloria Furman and Kathleen Nielson, along with a host of other talented writers, help us explore a vision-guided practice of our theology. Too often in church ministry, gender is received as a problem to be solved rather than as a beautiful gift from God to be explored. This book is a marvelous map to enjoy God, lead in God's church, and explore God's world, whether a woman is stepping into ministry for the first time or is a seasoned veteran."

Daniel Montgomery, Pastor, Sojourn Community Church, Louisville, Kentucky; Founder, Sojourn Network; author, *Faithmapping* and *Proof*

Word-Filled Women's Ministry

Other Crossway titles by The Gospel Coalition

Don't Call It a Comeback: The Old Faith for a New Day, edited by Kevin DeYoung (2011)

God's Love Compels Us: Taking the Gospel to the World, edited by D. A. Carson and Kathleen B. Nielson (2015)

The Gospel as Center: Renewing Our Faith and Reforming Our Ministry Practices, edited by D. A. Carson and Timothy Keller (2012)

Here Is Our God: God's Revelation of Himself in Scripture, edited by Kathleen B. Nielson and D. A. Carson (2014)

His Mission: Jesus in the Gospel of Luke, edited by D. A. Carson and Kathleen B. Nielson (2015)

The Scriptures Testify about Me: Jesus and the Gospel in the Old Testament, edited by D. A. Carson (2013)

Word-Filled — WOMEN'S MINISTRY

LOVING AND
SERVING
THE CHURCH

GLORIA FURMAN & KATHLEEN B. NIELSON

EDITORS

CROSSWAY

WHEATON, ILLINOIS

Library of Congress Cataloging-in-Publication Data
Word-filled women's ministry : loving and serving
the church / Gloria Furman and Kathleen B. Nielson,
editors ; foreword by Don Carson.
    pages cm
    "The Gospel Coalition."
    Includes bibliographical references and index.
    ISBN 978-1-4335-4523-8 (tp)
    1. Church work with women. I. Furman, Gloria,
1980– joint editor.
BV4445.W67   2017
253.082—dc23   2015000581

We dedicate this book to the Word-filled women
who have taught us and shown us
the love of Jesus Christ.

Contents

Foreword

Of the various components that make up the ministry of The Gospel Coalition, one of the most vibrant is the Women's Conference. This has served, among other things, to bring together a remarkable group of women who have studied Scripture and shared their experiences and then branched out into a growing list of shared projects. Not a few of these have been tied to writing and publishing.

In this book, ten of these women attractively encourage a broad range of ministries—ministries that are grounded in Scripture but that never forget there are real people out there. The title and subtitle hold up their twin foci: Word-filled ministry and the centrality of the local church. But what is most attractive about these essays is that they are wonderfully outward looking. They are thoughtful, but there is no trace of the kind of introspection that is essentially self-consuming. Out of both biblical conviction and years of experience, these women think seriously about discipleship, evangelism, inter-generational mentoring, and compassion. Their strength is evident; their commitment to Scripture robust; their joy in the gospel intoxicating; their anticipation of the consummation providing a lodestar to their lives and service.

Although this is a book by women to foster Word-filled women's ministry, much of it will be read with equal profit by men. I hope that some of those men will be pastors who, in consequence, reflect on what they can do to encourage such ministry in their own churches.

Don Carson

Introduction

Profitable ministry among women is grounded in God's Word, grows in the context of God's people, and aims for the glory of Christ. That's the premise of this book in a nutshell. It seems plain. And yet we have many questions to ask and much progress to make.

Ever since Eve, it has been our human tendency to distance ourselves from God's Word. No ministry in the church is exempt from the temptation to focus more on human desires and needs than on God's provision in his revelation of himself to us. Women's ministry in particular can so easily be all about women rather than being all about women together hearing and following God's voice, revealed in his Word.

The basic fact of God's creation of us as male and female lies at the heart of some of the greatest happiness and the greatest perversions of our human existence. How we flourish as male and female either clarifies or distorts the image of God in us and the glory of Christ we're meant to shine forth with joy. The subject of ministry among women, then, is not all about meeting women's needs; it's ultimately about God's glory.

Until we see that glory face-to-face, it is revealed to us in the Scriptures. This book starts and ends with affirmation of God's living and active Word as the lamp that lights every step in all of life—including in women's ministry. If the God of the universe does indeed speak to us in his Word, then our lives must be centered on hearing and living that Word—including in women's ministry. The Word shows us Jesus from beginning to end; so women's ministry must be from start to finish all about exalting Christ, our redeemer and Lord. In this book we will take time to establish this Word-based foundation in Christ, showing that women's ministry on this foundation not only helps women know and serve women, but most basically it helps women together know and serve the triune God.

The Bible calls believers to live within a particular context: that of God's people, known in the flesh through local congregations with local leaders. Many today, and certainly women today, confront ever-increasing temptations to minister to one another and alongside one another apart from this context. It can be a lot less messy just to do it ourselves. And we can actually do a really good job of it. Many of the chapters in this book—not just the one directly treating this topic—somehow find a way to bring up the importance of the church, the body of Christ in which God calls his people to find their identity and root their service. Even as we celebrate all sorts of old and new ways for ministry to happen among women, we must do our celebrating within the body of God's worshiping people and their carefully appointed leaders.

Increased separation from physical leadership has come matched with increased separation from biblical teaching, including teaching about men's and women's roles in the church and in the home; such separation threatens to tear women's ministry from a clear biblical context. The danger here is not just that we might get our doctrine wrong. The danger is that we might dim the image of God and the glory of Christ we're meant to shine forth with joy, in all our various pathways. The *opportunity* here is that we get to spur one another on in joyful obedience to the Word, for the sake of the gospel.

What better voices to add to the ongoing conversation on these issues than those of biblically committed women! How better to address not just the problems but also the possibilities of ministry among women than with the testimonies of those who are in the thick of it. The women represented in this volume (both the ones writing and the ones interviewed) speak from experience in studying and teaching the Word with women—and from a whole variety of contexts in which they love and serve the church. They know personally the issues addressed in these chapters. They have actively sought a place of flourishing within the church as leaders themselves who embrace the leadership of ordained men: the book explores women's ministry in what is often referred to as a *complementarian* context (as explained in chapter 2)—although we trust the book can benefit multiple contexts. These women come from various age groups, denominations, personal situations, and parts of the world, but they love and serve the same Jesus. They care about his glory more than anything, and so they care for women in the eternally best way—not each the same way, and none perfectly or without struggle, to be sure, but all for their Savior's sake.

These women's voices weave together richly—in part 1 (three chapters) focusing on the Word at the heart of women's ministry; in part 2 (three chapters) focusing on contexts for women's ministry, starting with the local church and reaching out to the world; in part 3 (three chapters) focusing on specific issues related to women's ministry. The concluding chapter reminds us what we're ultimately aiming for, as we minister. You'll hear these voices landing on certain key themes, weaving together strands of similar colors. We've relished bringing together these voices, each so distinct and yet all in harmony because of hearts that beat with a common gospel rhythm.

This book offers not an exhaustive but an accelerated discussion of women's ministry—through making public some voices of women involved in doing it. It offers not a formula but rather a solid set of biblical markers for the road ahead in ministry among women. The Word tells us that along this road of ministry we can expect to find all the nations of the world streaming to Christ. Our goal is to encourage women to join that stream and help it grow. Our ultimate goal in ministry among women is the glory of Jesus Christ.

Gloria Furman

Kathleen Nielson

PART 1

THE HEART
OF WOMEN'S
MINISTRY

— 1 —

The Word at the Center

Hearing God Speak

Kathleen Nielson

What pictures do the words "women's ministry" bring to mind? We come from different contexts, all of us. Some will picture a small circle of jean-clad women gathered at a friend's kitchen table or maybe sitting on folding chairs in a church meeting room. Others will recall crucial conversations one-to-one at a local coffee shop. Others will think of regular visits by a younger woman to an older one too feeble to leave her cramped, old-photo–filled apartment. Others will be carried back to times of crisis, with a few women gathered in a friend's living room, prayers and tears flowing. Others will see lovely teas with flowers on tablecloths and perfumed women dressed in colors that match the flowers. For some, the scene may be a church kitchen, where women with flushed, focused faces are wearing oven mitts to handle steaming pans. Others may envision classrooms, with women leaning over chattering children in little chairs around low tables, or auditoriums filled with rows of attentive women listening to a woman up front standing behind a podium. And others will have entirely different sets of pictures—these are just a few from my set!

How can we gather all our varied pictures into one album we might legitimately title "women's ministry"? There would never be enough pages—or gigabytes. And that is a good thing. This book addresses women's ministry not simply as specific ministry *programs* but also as an ongoing flow of ministry happening in diverse ways among women in local church congregations. Our question: How can we encourage that flow to be strong and full of life—and how can we begin to talk about that flow in any way coherently? How? Only through a central focus on the Word of God.

All our various snapshots will come together if we see each of these scenes as a place where Word work is happening. Might we imagine each of these pictures of women (and many more) super-imposed on a background page filled with the words of Scripture? Women's ministry must be first and foremost grounded in the Word. We must not start with the needs of women—although we must get to those needs. As in the case of any church ministry, in women's ministry we must start with the Word of God at the heart of everything we do.

To talk about the Scriptures as central, I will start with and keep returning to Isaiah 55, for that chapter tells us why we need God's Word. This will not be a thorough exposition, but as we move through the sections of Isaiah 55, my aim is to let its powerful words point us to basic truths about God's Word that must shape all our lives and ministries, as followers of Jesus Christ.

GOD'S WORD IS GOD SPEAKING

Let's start at the center of the chapter. I don't think there are any more beautiful verses than Isaiah 55:10–11 to help us grasp the foundational truth that *the Bible is God speaking to us.* It might seem hard to believe, when we think about it: here we are in Isaiah listening to a prophet who brought God's Word to God's people more than seven hundred years before Christ, in a divided kingdom that was in decline and heading for disaster. These words are thousands of years old, written down by a prophet who is long gone. And yet we believers claim to stake our lives on these words and others like them, putting our hope in the clear central message of Isaiah's book: *the Lord saves his people.* How do we so trust these ancient words? Here is God's Word on God's word:

> For as the rain and the snow come down from heaven
>> and do not return there but water the earth,
> making it bring forth and sprout,
>> giving seed to the sower and bread to the eater,
> so shall my word be that goes out from my mouth;
>> it shall not return to me empty,
> but it shall accomplish that which I purpose,
>> and shall succeed in the thing for which I sent it.
>> (Isa. 55:10–11)

The first truth to affirm about the Bible is that *it is God speaking.* It's not just a book about God. What's the picture Isaiah uses for God's Word? It's a picture of rain and snow coming down from heaven, giving life to the earth and making things grow. It's a picture of a heavenly gift—a gift that comes, remarkably enough, *from God's mouth.*

Isaiah's picture corrects a lot of misconceptions. So many voices these days tell us that in order to get at truth, we have to look deep inside ourselves, or at least we have to start there. But this picture shows us something originating from far outside ourselves—like precipitation from the sky, something we desperately need but don't have in ourselves—so that we're called not to look inward to receive it but to look outward, to look *up* and hold out our hands.

Many reading this book may be noticing a growing general tendency these days to focus on our own personal experience in our thinking and in our speaking—and even in our Bible study. That tendency, of course, is as old as Eve, who was attracted by the tantalizing taste of that fruit in her mouth, the delight of that fruit right in front of her eyes, and the allure of that fruit that would make her wise (see Gen. 3:6). Eve was drawn by the Serpent into evil through a focus on her own sensations, desires, and self-perceptions—as opposed to a focus on the clear word of God that he had spoken.

Certain kinds of phrases float regularly by women in particular these days, calling women to *pay attention to who they are, release their God-given potential, listen to their longings for significance, embrace their doubts, dream the dreams in their hearts,* and so forth. Such inner journeys can sometimes be good and necessary. It is perhaps important to say that such an emphasis might represent a pent-up reaction to older generations' overemphasis on outward propriety as opposed to inward transparency and transformation.

The call not to neglect our inner experience is a valid one, but everything turns on the question of whose voice is directing us, whether it be our own or the voices around us or the voice of God given to us in his Word. In our thirst for deeply personal meaning, we can forget how deeply personal are the Scriptures. Sometimes the voices around us talk about the Bible as a textbook for theological formulas that we have to learn, as if for a test in school. And so we might think of taking in the Scriptures as a dry, academic thing—and we'd really rather do something warm and personal.

This is a perennial struggle in women's Bible study circles. Two distinct sorts of camps seem to develop: Shall we be warm and welcoming and personal, or shall we be academic and study the text? What an unfortunate distinction! Here's the question: What could be more personal than feeling the very breath of God—actually hearing him speak? According to 2 Timothy 3:16, all Scripture is inspired, or *breathed out*, by God. Isaiah, in delivering God's word, proclaimed this very truth about the very word he was delivering: it *goes out from God's mouth* (55:11). Indeed, all the words of the collected canonical texts are the very breath of God's mouth— breathed by his Spirit through the minds and imaginations of the authors who wrote them, who "spoke from God as they were carried along by the Holy Spirit" (2 Pet. 1:21). This is about as personal as it gets: the very breath of God from the mouth of God, received by the people of God. In the Old Testament the very same Hebrew word is translated both "breath" and "spirit." God's word is alive with his breath, his very Spirit.

I love the way respected theologian John Frame puts it at the start of his theologically weighty work called *The Doctrine of the Word of God*. To understand how the Bible works, according to Dr. Frame, you should imagine God standing at the foot of your bed at night talking to you.[1] Imagine—the God of the universe speaking right to you. It's that personal.

Our God is a speaking God. How did God create the world? By speaking. He said, "Let there be light" (Gen. 1:3), and there was light, not after but *in the speaking of the words*. God's word gave form and shape to the earth; his word holds everything together— including us. You and I were made to take in God's breath, through his Word, and so to live in relationship with him. That relationship was broken in the fall—as sin came in and separated us from our holy creator God. But he restores that relationship by giving us his Word, ultimately his Word made flesh; we'll see Isaiah 55 pointing us toward that restoration found only in Jesus Christ.

Why does Isaiah use all these pictures like rain, snow, seeds, and bread? This is not abstract theology, is it? This living Word is as real as the bread we enjoy for breakfast and through which our bodies are energized. This is personal truth—as personal as feeling some-one's breath on your face, or looking up into a pelt of snowflakes from the clouds, or watching the rain fall on your wilting flowers and seeing them straighten up and stretch toward the sky. These vivid pictures communicate the wonder of the way God speaks to us from heaven, sending his own word from outside us, in order to give us life we do not have within ourselves.

If the Bible really is God speaking, then it follows that each of us human beings needs more than anything else in the world to look up and receive this Word, every day of our lives. This is our logical response and our most basic need, both as individuals and as God's people together. We need to stand under the preaching and teaching of the Word like the parched earth waiting under the heavens for rain to come down. It is beautiful to look over a church congrega-tion attentively listening to a sermon and to sense the life-giving watering that is happening as the Word is preached and people's souls start straightening up and stretching toward heaven. Ideally, this process of watering happens in every part of church life: in small groups, classes, one-to-one conversations and counseling—at the heart of all the various ministries of a congregation of people who acknowledge the Bible as God's Word that comes from God's mouth. This is an urgent truth, that God's Word is God speaking. This truth must shape the lives and ministries of God's people.

GOD'S WORD IS POWERFUL

The second truth to affirm about the Bible is that *it is powerful*. It must be, if it is the very breath of God, the breath that made the whole world. This is what Isaiah 55:11 is talking about when it says that God's word will not return to him empty but will accomplish that which he purposes; it will do everything God intends it to do. Unlike our words, God's words are always linked with actual real-ity; in fact, they make happen everything that happens. Many of us memorized the apostle Paul's words to Timothy, in 2 Timothy 3:16, where first we hear that "all Scripture is breathed out by God," and then right away we find the most amazing claims about all the areas to which God applies the power of his Word: teaching, reproof, correction, training in righteousness—making the man of God competent, equipped for every—think of it, *every* good work! God's Word is powerful enough to be comprehensively equipping; this is his intention, and he will accomplish it. On that truth we can build our ministries in the church.

But we need to read the previous verse as well, 2 Timothy 3:15, where Paul makes the huge claim that the sacred writings God inspired are "able to make you wise for salvation through faith in Christ Jesus." God's words actually call us from death to life, first of all; they have that much power, as God's Spirit applies them. This makes me think of the words of Jesus to his friend Lazarus who had died. Do you recall the scene, as Jesus stood before the tomb of Lazarus and said two little words: "Come out!" (John 11:43)? And Lazarus came out, from death to life. That's how God's Word works. It accomplishes what he purposes. It succeeds in the thing for which he sends it. It calls people to life in Christ and then trains them, comprehensively, how to live in Christ.

If this Word is that powerful, then it follows that we can trust it. We can trust this powerful Word to do its work among God's people. This means we will make our plans based on the fact that this Word is "living and active, sharper than any two-edged sword." We will not sheathe this sword in the various ministries of our churches, but we will draw it eagerly, exposing young and old to those sharp edges that pierce "to the division of soul and of spirit, of joints and of marrow, . . . discerning the thoughts and intentions of the heart" (Heb. 4:12). We have no such power in ourselves; we need "the sword of the Spirit" (Eph. 6:17), whose cut is life-saving and life-sustaining.

What might it mean to *sheathe* (cover, put away) this sword among God's people? Perhaps this happens most often when we simply don't take time to hear and study its words or to help others do so. Maybe we're just talking about its principles, or simply using various texts as jumping-off points to talk about our own ideas or about what we think the people we're addressing need to hear. Maybe we're spending more time together reading books about the Bible than reading the Bible itself. Maybe we think a lively video will draw people more regularly than the live teaching of the Word. We often simply do not trust the power of God's breathed-out Word to bring people to life, lead people to healing and hope, and train them comprehensively for godly living.

What will it mean, more positively, to unsheathe this sword? How can we draw it out into the open and let it shine and do its work, as we minister to and along with others? We know we must trust that by his Spirit, through his Word, God will accomplish his purposes without fail. Our trust must certainly be a *respectful* trust—like we have for a powerful weapon such as a sharp, two-edged sword that we'd better learn how to handle rightly. We have to learn how it works. For the Bible, that means learning how it speaks—in whole books, from Genesis to Revelation, and in distinct genres, from narrative to poetry to prophecy to apocalyptic. The penetration of the Word surely happens most deeply when we allow it to speak in the form in which it has been given to us, rather than dicing it up and extracting segments or bending it to our own purposes. Not only from the pulpit but in every area of church life and ministry we can aim to let the Word have its full say as we listen fully, not neglecting any part of all the Spirit-inspired Scriptures.

Do we think our youth need to learn about marriage and sex from a biblical perspective? Well, then, of course it is fine and good to have topical seminars and invite in expert speakers on the subject. But how crucial to address such issues in the context of a steady, purposeful teaching through the books of God's Word. Our youth will be better prepared through receiving not just answers to certain hard issues but a way of dealing biblically with hard issues, as we spread out the fabric of biblical thinking and see all the issues of our lives as threads in the Bible's story of redemption centered in Christ. If the Word is a dry set of propositions we have to enliven, then of course this will not work. If the Word is God speaking to us personally and powerfully, then of course this will not only work but will be our only reasonable course of action.

For women, it is good indeed to have studies and seminars on all sorts of topics related to sex and marriage and womanhood and roles of men and women in the church and on and on. But how crucial to be addressing these important topics also in the context of a steady, purposeful teaching through the books of God's Word. If that kind of teaching happens on every level of a church congregation, then we dense human beings (I address myself!) might begin to get it—to get the way the sword of the Word penetrates deeply into all of life. We will begin to understand the Bible's teaching about women and men as part of a whole story of God's redeeming a people for himself in Christ. We will understand Titus's instruction about older women teaching younger in the context of a unified epistle celebrating the necessary connection in the church between good doctrine and good works. We will take in the Word more comprehensively as we hear it prayed and taught and studied in the voices of not just pastors but also other men and women and children.

GOD'S WORD IS FOR EVERYONE

This brings us to the third truth to be affirmed about the Word: *it is for everyone*. Not especially for certain ones but for everyone. Sometimes the voices around us will make us think that maybe just the really smart people can really understand the Bible, or the pastors or those with extensive theological education, or the people who've been good or who grew up in nice Christian families, or maybe the men who are called to lead their families. We might even think of such things as a kind of down payment, in order to qualify—and some people seem richer than others.

The people of Israel back in Isaiah's day tended to think like this as well: they were God's chosen people; God had given *them* his Word and his promises of great blessing, even of a great king in the line of David who would rule forever. In Isaiah 54, the chapter before the one we're considering, God makes amazing promises to his people, promises of unfailing love and a shining city and blessed children and safety from all enemies (vv. 9–14). That surely made the people of Judah, with Jerusalem as its capital city, feel pretty special. The prophet Isaiah *is* indeed bringing God's word to Judah, which will go through terrible destruction but which will be wonderfully reestablished. But these verses also reach out into layers of fulfillment, as Isaiah, carried along by the Spirit, speaks out to an audience much wider than he knew—in fact, as wide as the whole earth, which will be renewed for God's people from all the nations.

We started in the center of Isaiah 55, but let's notice how that chapter begins—with a call to come *drink*, and come *eat* (see vv. 1–3a). But to whom does this call go out, in the opening verse? To Judah? No—to "everyone who thirsts." The only explicit qualification here is to be thirsty. The only other qualification seems to be that you mustn't have money to pay for what you're supposed to buy. This sounds totally illogical. It doesn't make sense to come buy food and drink if you have no money. But Isaiah is emphatic that those with lots of money are buying all the wrong things.

Isaiah loves pictures, and this poetry is full of them. How does this one work? The food and drink give us a picture of *what*? Isaiah tells us, after he's captured our attention with this dramatic call. He gives us God's own words, there in the middle of verse 2: "*Listen*

diligently to me, and eat what is good." Verse 3: "*Incline your e*
and come to me; *hear*, that your soul may live." We can't help but
notice the repeated commands: *Listen . . . incline your ear . . . hear.*
In other words, eating is a picture of listening to God, and food and
drink picture God's Word that we take in. It's the sustenance each
one of us needs. His Word is the living water and the bread of life,
delivered through the Spirit. It's not for those who think they have
some standing before God by being smart or good or rich or in the
right family or anything else; it's for every thirsty one who realizes
the complete lack of any ability to pay for the life God pours out in
us, only by his grace. The rain of God's Word falls down in all the
cracks and crevices, and on every plant and every blade of grass—
calling *everyone* who's thirsty.

Because God calls every thirsty one to hear, then he must intend
for every thirsty one to be able to understand. And we've seen that
God's Word accomplishes all that he intends. So it follows that we
can expect understanding of this Word! Not completely, of course—
but more and more, the more any one of us studies and listens and
learns and prays. The more we look up and hold out our hands. This
is a lifelong activity. It can be hard work. In the end, understanding
depends not on us but on God's Spirit, who inspired the words to
begin with. The beauty is that as we listen, and as preachers preach
and teachers teach and thirsty people help each other come drink, by
the help of the Spirit, the Bible doesn't hide its truth; no—it lights up!

The reformers of the 1500s based their lives and work on this
truth, which they called the "perspicuity" of Scripture, meaning the
understandability of Scripture. Men like Martin Luther and William
Tyndale believed that God's Word should be read and studied by
all, translated into the common language, available to every person
to hear and learn—not just held in the hands of an elite group who
would interpret it for everybody else. The perspicuity of Scripture
is a beautiful doctrine, one that people have fought and died for,

 ̣ould give us hope, both as we read and study the
 e share it with others—others in our own culture and
 r the world. The Word of God speaks clearly into the
wh⌐ ̣ he made.

GOD'S WORD IS ALL ABOUT JESUS

We've said that the Bible is God speaking, that it is powerful, and that it is for everyone. But we're left with a question here in Isaiah 55. How are we told to "buy" this food and drink? How can it be bought without money? What, then, is the payment, and who pays? Verse 3 of Isaiah 55 continues with the best news of the whole chapter. It's the news we're called to hear and eat. It's that which God purposes, the thing for which he sends his word. It's the news about God's covenant promise given through King David.

All through the Old Testament, as far back as Adam and Eve, God doesn't stop talking to us. He doesn't leave us alone in our sin, as we deserve. No, he comes, and he speaks. He makes promises and covenants that unfold—from Adam and Eve through Abraham down through King David—promises of a seed that would bring blessing to the whole earth. To King David, God promised a great, eternal king to come in his line (2 Sam. 7:8–17). The prophet Isaiah talks a lot about these promises, and chapter 55 offers a vivid example. In these next verses we hear God himself speaking of his promises to his people, first referring to his covenant with King David. But as God talks about David, something amazing happens: attention turns from the human King David, who received the covenant, to the son of David promised by the covenant. By verse 5, God in effect turns and actually speaks to the promised Son of David, his own Son:

> And I will make with you an everlasting covenant,
>> my steadfast, sure love for David.

Behold, I made him a witness to the peoples,
    a leader and commander for the peoples.
Behold, you shall call a nation that you do not know,
    and a nation that did not know you shall run to you,
because of the LORD your God, and of the Holy One of Israel,
    for he has glorified you. (vv. 3b–5)

The fourth truth is the truth of the whole Scripture: it's that *the Bible is all about Jesus*. Here we are in this Old Testament prophecy to the nation of Judah, and what's Isaiah doing? He's calling everybody who's thirsty to come and hear the good news of God's everlasting covenant with David. David here prefigures, or points ahead to, the promised king to come in his line—the one who will indeed be a witness and a leader and commander (v. 4) not just for a people but for "the peoples," *many* peoples, in fact all the nations of the earth. Verse 5 declares to this promised one that he will call a foreign nation, one Israel does not know and that does not know Israel. We're reading here a confirmation of the promise to Abraham that all the nations of the world would be blessed through his seed (Gen. 12:3). The promises came *through* Israel, but they didn't come only *to* Israel; they came through Israel to the whole wide earth—just as God promised. And all God's promises pointed to his Son, Jesus Christ, born of the seed of Abraham, in the line of David.

These verses are just one example of the way Isaiah's prophecy reaches forward to Jesus the Messiah, promised king descended from David. We tend to quote Isaiah's more well-known prophecies, those of the suffering servant—which actually come in the chapters leading right up to this one. Many of us treasure those poignant prophecies of the suffering servant from Isaiah 53, the one who bore our griefs and carried our sorrows (v. 4). That suffering servant *is* the promised king we're reading about here just two chapters later, in this climactic chapter of Isaiah's middle section. The promised servant came, suffered God's judgment in our place on the cross, paid the price for our salvation, and then rose from the dead and ascended in glory to reign and to draw all the nations to himself. This is the *glorified* one prophetically addressed in verse 5. He is the answer to the question of how this food and drink are bought: not *by us* who have no money but *for* us, by the one who paid the price for us. Jesus is the answer to the thirst that Isaiah 55 talks about—and it's the same thirst Jesus himself was talking about when he told the Samaritan woman at the well that he would give her living water so that she'd never be thirsty again (John 4:14). Jesus has always been the source of this living water.

If we are thinking about Word-based ministry, we are thinking about ministry that opens up for people the big story of the Scriptures with Jesus at the center, so that they can understand the stories of their own lives as centered in the story and the glory of Jesus. It revolutionizes our perspective to take in the overarching storyline of the Scriptures, starting in the beginning and seeing there in the beginning the Word that was with God and in fact was God—this Word through whom all things were created (John 1:1–3). What a story, which begins with this God creating the heavens and the earth and ends with God *re*-creating, making a *new* heaven and a *new* earth. The story holds together from beginning to end. It begins in a beautiful place where the tree of life grows and where human beings live in communion with God—a place quickly lost, as sin breaks that communion. But then the promised Christ finally comes to restore that communion, as through his death God redeems a people for himself from all the nations of the earth. The Bible even lets us glimpse the finale, that new heaven and earth, again with the tree of life, where God again dwells with his people, with the risen Christ at the center, the Lamb on the throne.

Each one of us would like to make the story all about "me." Indeed, many voices around encourage us to see ourselves as the center of the narrative. That's why, when we go to the Scriptures, we tend to ask first what the text means to us—how it makes us feel, how it can help us. When we shape a ministry, we tend to ask first how that ministry can meet the needs of the particular group involved. That is not a bad question. But what if, instead of starting with that question, we started by asking how that group can best be taking in the Scriptures so that they can understand their own stories in light of the big story of God's creating a people for himself through his Son? According to the Scriptures, how can that group be all about the story and the glory of Christ, who shines through the Scriptures from beginning to end?

The voices out there will ask: "Can't we just be all about loving and serving Jesus in our ministry?" Yes, but what does it mean to love and serve Jesus? Who is Jesus? How do we best love and serve him? There will be as many different answers to these questions as there are groups of people until we take our questions to the Word of God. The Scriptures tell us clearly who Jesus is, and it's a quite different description from the various ones floating around in the culture, even the evangelical culture. To get the whole story of Jesus, we must be regularly reading and teaching the whole book—New Testament and Old, narrative, poetry, Gospels, apocalyptic, Epistles, Wisdom Literature, prophecy—all of it! All the parts work together, in God's providence, to feed us fully on this one who comes and tells us that he is the living water and the bread of life.

GOD'S WORD IS A MATTER OF LIFE AND DEATH

What comes next in Isaiah 55 is important. Without these verses we could believe all the rest of the chapter, but we wouldn't have to do anything about it. Verses 6–9 tell us that *the Word is a matter of life and death*. They are kind of like the altar call of Isaiah 55:

Seek the LORD while he may be found;
  call upon him while he is near;

> let the wicked forsake his way,
>   and the unrighteous man his thoughts;
> let him return to the LORD, that he may have
>   compassion on him,
>   and to our God, for he will abundantly pardon.
> For my thoughts are not your thoughts,
>   neither are your ways my ways, declares the LORD.
> For as the heavens are higher than the earth,
>   so are my ways higher than your ways
> and my thoughts than your thoughts. (vv. 6–9)

There's a life-and-death urgency here. Time will run out. It's clear that this opportunity to hear is offered only while God "may be found," or "while he is near." It's clear that the offer involves not just being happy or prosperous; we've already heard (back in v. 3) that the life of our souls is at stake. The opposite of pardon (v. 7) is condemnation. And we're in a desperate position, because the word we need is so high we can't reach it. Verses 8 and 9 make clear that God and we exist in two different realms, and God's is too high for us. Verse 9 leaves us hopelessly cut off: "For as the heavens are higher than the earth, so are my ways higher than your ways and my thoughts than your thoughts."

Now that we've worked our way from the beginning of the chapter to those magnificent verses with which we began, we can see why verse 10 begins with the word "For." It's continuing the "For" of verse 9 and the "For" of verse 8, and the huge, growing point is that we by ourselves cannot get at this desperately needed word; we have to receive it from heaven. Seeing verses 8 and 9, we grasp even more of the wonder of verses 10 and 11, that God's words, from which we're cut off, should come down to us like the rain and snow from heaven to give us life as opposed to death. How amazing. How merciful.

All the other religions of the world involve a reaching up to heaven, in order to attain a higher level of righteousness, a raising up of ourselves. The Bible reveals a God who comes near to us as he bids us come and who sends down from heaven his word—ultimately the Word made flesh, his very Son. We Christians indeed have good news, urgent news, life-and-death news to receive and to offer through this Word, which has come down to us. If the Word is what it says it is, then as it rains into our lives we believers should surely be brimming with the urgency of hearing and sharing its merciful good news in these last days while the Lord may still be found.

It follows, then, that in our lives and ministries, we will be actively responding to and calling others to respond to God's Word. Such active response involves, first of all, a more integrated evangelistic thrust to our ministries than we perhaps routinely imagine. Chapter 5 of this book addresses this topic specifically, but in many of the chapters comes a repeated challenge to think of ministry among women not as a program that holds an evangelistic event from time to time, but rather as a network of relationships that is always reaching out by means of the living Word—in our Bible studies, our friendships and mentoring, all our gatherings—always reaching out to help others receive the life-giving Word from which we would all be cut off had it not come down to us. If a ministry is filled with focused study and teaching of the Word, then it's actually difficult for this *not* to happen, because God's Word is both sufficient and effective for our salvation and sanctification.

Active response to the Word involves not just receiving and sharing the gospel but also living it out more and more faithfully. The good news, which is a matter of life and death, is news that comprehensively transforms life as God's people are conformed to the image of his Son. Notice that this passage speaks of both *thoughts* and *ways* (v. 9). Isaiah combines the taking in of God's Word with the doing of it. The four verbs in verses 6 and 7 offer a progression of imperatives, or commands, which are almost like a trail of footsteps to follow. In verse 6, "seek" and "call" command a response to God's Word that first turns toward him (*seek*) and then speaks back to him with our own words (*call*). He's a God of words, and he made us creatures of words in his own image, so that we can actually answer his words and connect to him with ours.

The next two commands, "forsake" and "return" (v. 7), call for a turning away from evil and turning to the Lord himself, who pardons that evil when we repent. This call echoes loudly both for unbelievers, who must repent, and for believers, who have heard God's voice and repented but have not perfectly followed that voice (as none of us will, until we see Jesus face-to-face). To *seek* and *call* and *forsake* and *return* are actions we must take initially, as we respond in faith to God's regenerating call on our hearts—but also continually, as the Spirit keeps applying the Word to our hearts.

These verses keep speaking to all of us. They call us to turn *from* our own thoughts and ways *to* God's thoughts and ways. This is what the Word teaches us to do as we listen to it, taking in its life and being changed in both our thoughts and our ways. We study and teach the Bible throughout our various ministries not just in order to become knowledgeable but to have our lives transformed and ever in the process of being transformed—until we die or Jesus comes again and the process is complete. What will this look like in our ministries as, by the Spirit through the Word, we actively respond and help others to respond in life-changing ways? Hopefully these next chapters will begin to answer that question in relation to women's ministries. At the least we know it will mean a lot of seeking and calling upon the Lord and a lot of forsaking wicked ways and returning to the Lord.

What makes these actions good is not we who perform them but God, who both commands them and also enables them and who then responds to them. What a mercy to read that our God of *compassion* will not just pardon but *abundantly pardon* (v. 7). The rain does not just trickle; it pours out pardon on our dry and needy souls. This is good news indeed. Our places of ministry should be places where people are finding life—new life, and growing abundant life—because in his mercy the God of our salvation has come near. He has poured out life from himself in his Son by his Spirit through his Word.

GOD'S WORD IS BEAUTIFUL

Let's notice one more truth: *God's Word is beautiful.* Consider: just through this one chapter our minds have been filled with pictures and sensations of wine and milk and the most delightful rich food and rain and snow and healthy green plants and seeds and bread and on and on! God clearly aims to penetrate us with his Word not just through our minds but also through our imaginations and our emotions and our senses—through our whole beings. No part of the Bible is just bare propositional truth; all its words are, as the writer of Ecclesiastes says, weighed, shaped, and arranged with great care so that they are not just words of truth but also words of delight (12:9–10). The truth of God is beautiful. A grammatically complex sentence written by the apostle Paul is like a winding path with many branches, endlessly pleasing in the relation of all its different parts that lead us through the richness of gospel truth. We have been reading magnificent poetry in these words given to us by Isaiah, rich unfolding parallel lines full of images that show us God's amazing gift of gospel grace. *Every* kind of literature in the Bible has its own shape and beauty that call forth our notice and delight.

How can we mark our ministries not just with clear teaching of the Word but with delight in the Word? Actually, the clearer and more faithful our handling of the Scriptures, the more that handling *will* be characterized by delight. When we pay the closest attention to these God-breathed words, we will be noticing how they are put together. We will be distinguishing the diverse kinds of literature crafted by the various human writers who were carried along by the Holy Spirit to speak from God in their unique voices and contexts. We will be understanding more fully the Bible's ways of speaking and inevitably marveling at its beauty.

But its beauty is not simply the beauty of form in addition to content. Its beauty is the beauty of form and content so wonderfully wedded that when we diagram one of those complex Pauline sentences or unpack two parallel poetic lines, we will be delighting in the meaning, through the process of receiving it with an ultimately satisfying submission to the text. We will have listened diligently to the inspired words. It's a matter of opening our hands wide to receive the rich food or relish the life-giving rain. Of course, the more we delight in the Word, the more others will be drawn to hold out their hands as well. Coming together with delight around God's Word grows and builds up God's people in amazing ways.

The final verses of Isaiah 55 bring this chapter to a remarkably beautiful climax, picturing the results of all God's people and in fact all the earth fully receiving and celebrating God's Word:

> For you shall go out in joy
>   and be led forth in peace;
> the mountains and the hills before you
>   shall break forth into singing,
>   and all the trees of the field shall clap their hands.
> Instead of the thorn shall come up the cypress;
>   instead of the brier shall come up the myrtle;
> and it shall make a name for the Lord,
>   an everlasting sign that shall not be cut off. (vv. 12–13)

The *sprouting* we saw back in verse 10 bursts here into full and glorious bloom. These are results that we glimpse even now, in the body of Christ, but we know we'll see them fully and finally when

Jesus comes again and the story is complete. That's the goal to which these verses point, and so we learn here what should be the direction, the *momentum*, of our ministries, all of which form part of the flow of these last days heading toward Christ's appearing.

The book's final chapter will land us on this point, but it's good to affirm it from the start: our ministries exist not simply for the purpose of helping people live well now; our ministries, like our whole lives, must aim for the end, when we'll see Jesus face-to-face. The glorious pictures in Isaiah 55 all climax in one end: to "make a name for the LORD, / an everlasting sign that shall not be cut off" (v. 13). That name is the name of Jesus, to whom God has given "the name that is above every name, so that at the name of Jesus every knee should bow" (Phil. 2:9–10).

Even now, along the way, our ministries can be sprouting more and more with fruitful life as they find their center in the Word that mercifully rains down on us. We have nothing else on which we can eternally depend. That album of women's ministry with its varied pictures can become increasingly colorful and beautiful as it shows the process of opening ourselves to words from the very mouth of God, coming down to us like rain and snow from heaven, watering the earth, bringing forth life, accomplishing all that God purposes for the glory of his name.

— 2 —

The Word on Women

Enjoying Distinction

Claire Smith

The same day the invitation to contribute to this volume arrived in my in-box, a Sydney newspaper reported an online campaign to stop Australian toy manufacturers and retailers from targeting products as for girls or boys. They want toys grouped by themes, not "gender stereotypes."[1]

In one sense, this makes sense. Many boys enjoy dolls and playing kitchen; and girls (like me) enjoy model planes and cricket bats. But the campaigners' agenda is not just the removal of gender stereotypes. They want to stop *gender* being a major part of who a child is—who *we* are. They want a world in which a person's identity is not shaped by the first label we receive at birth: "It's a girl!" or "It's a boy!"[2]

They are not alone. Facebook has stopped offering only two

genders for users' profiles. As of this writing, it offers fifty-six different gender identities.[3]

These are just two examples of a growing trend that sees gender as a social construct: a phenomenon that is the product of social forces and the language we use to talk about life rather than something that is part of biologically determined reality. For an increasingly noisy, growing minority, it is a construct that has had its day.

Yet here *we* are writing, and here *you* are reading, a book about *women*: a book that claims not only that women exist but also that gender is an intrinsic and essential good and God-given part of who we are. So before we consider further the questions about ministry among women, we need first to understand what it is to be a woman (or a man) in God's purposes.

GOD CREATED MAN MALE AND FEMALE

As we saw in chapter 1, God's Word alone provides the foundation for faith and life, and the best place to begin to explore gender-related questions is the Bible's first three chapters, where (among other things) God gives us a lesson in biblical anthropology: an introduction to *who we are*.

Genesis begins not with one creation account but with two complementary accounts (Gen. 1:1–2:3; 2:4–25). Both deal with God's creation of all things, but they give different views and focus on complementary truths. They're not conflicting accounts, but they're not carbon copies either. Each teaches the same and different truths about God, creation, and humankind.

Both accounts reveal God as sovereign creator, loving ruler and lawgiver. He is there before anything else. He sees all things, knows all things, and creates all things. He is generous and good. He is over creation, speaking it into existence (Genesis 1), and he is present in it, forming, planting, and giving life (Genesis 2).

In both accounts, chaos and formlessness are replaced by order, distinction, purpose, and productivity. God is always separate and distinct from creation. He rules over it and is present in it, but he is not in or part of anything that is made.

Yet remarkably, when we come to the pinnacle of his creative work—"man" or humankind—we find that the Creator shares his divine image with his creatures (Gen. 1:26–27; Gen. 9:5–6). They correspond to him and so relate to him as no other creature does. They are his face to his creation, made in his image to tend and govern as his representatives.

But they are not genderless humans; they are *male* or *female* humans. One humanity in two kinds, both equally made and delighted in by God. Both equally bear the divine image. Both are charged with filling the earth and subduing it as God's representatives. But they are decidedly different: male *or* female.[4]

Now, you don't need me to tell you that God made the birds and bees and most other creatures male and female too, but in Genesis we're left to assume that. Not so for humans! Our sexual differentiation is mentioned because it is significant. For one thing, it leads into God's command that humans must be fruitful and multiply and make more image bearers to extend God's rule throughout all creation (Gen. 1:28).

But our sexual differences also help tell us who we are, as human beings created in God's image. We have to take care how we understand this. I once heard someone say that God made humanity male and female because God is male and female. This is not what the Bible teaches. Being made in the image of God has something to do with humans being male and female, but it is not because God is male and female.

God is spirit (John 4:24) and does not have gender as we have gender. Scripture sometimes uses feminine imagery to describe God,[5] but God has revealed himself as Father, Son (who became the man, Jesus Christ), and Spirit (who is the Spirit of the Father and the Son), and we can know God only as he has revealed himself. It is right, then, to use male pronouns and titles for God and not to ignore his self-revelation.[6] At the same time, though, God is not male as men and boys are male.

Nevertheless, Genesis tells us that whatever else being made in God's image means for humanity—our role as his representatives; our capacity for moral judgment, relationships, creativity, and so on—it also involves being created male and female. We get a hint of how this is so when God says, "Let *us* make man in *our* image" (Gen. 1:26), and then the writer adds: "in the image of God he created him; male and female he created them" (v. 27). The apostle Paul does a similar thing when he links gender differences with our creation in God's image and places his discussion in the theological context of the ordered relations within the Godhead (1 Cor. 11:3, cf. 11:7–8, 12).[7] Being made in God's image and being male and female are connected.

The relationship of male and female—a relationship of unity and differentiation of the nonidentical but equal parts of the one humanity—in some way reflects the perfect unity and differentiation of the eternal persons of the triune God: one God in three persons, equal in divinity and personhood, who love and act and relate in perfect unity.

Yet despite this equality and unity, the divine persons are not interchangeable; neither are their relations or functions. The Father is the Father and not the Son or the Spirit. The Son is the Son, not the Father, and so on. Moreover, the Father sends the Son, not the Son the Father. The Son is begotten of the Father, not the Father of the Son. The Son was incarnate, not the Father or the Spirit. Unity and differentiation. Sameness and difference. And *order without inequality*. All these are true of the triune God.

Likewise, male and female are equal in humanity, dignity, worth, and purpose but not identical, and, whether or not we are married, our differences work together to create relationships of unity and complementarity. We are not simply persons. We are *male* or *female* persons made for human society, built through relationships with people of both genders.

Current trends about human sexuality should not surprise us. Just as our face or image doesn't remain on the mirror when we turn away, modern notions of gender diversity and plasticity, and the same-sex/queer agenda are simply expressions of our society's turning away from the one in whose image we are made. As we forget God, we lose our identity. But the fact remains: God made us with binary gender polarity, and it is a good and *God*-given part of our identity.

NEITHER MALE NOR FEMALE BUT ALL ONE IN CHRIST JESUS

Yet some Christians—even some evangelicals—have come to see the biblical differences between men and women as a consequence of sin rather than as part of God's original design. These differences then belong to fallen humanity and are overcome or reversed in Christ. The text typically used is Galatians 3:28, where Paul writes: "There is neither Jew nor Greek, there is neither slave nor free, there is no male and female, for you are all one in Christ Jesus."

The argument goes something like this: the gospel challenges and overturns those things that create divisions and hierarchies in fallen human society. Therefore, while biological differences remain, all role distinctions between men and women are removed in Christ, and men and women without distinction can take on the same roles and do the same things in society, church, and marriage.

This sounds reasonable to some because it contains an element of truth. In Christ, the deep divisions in human society have been overcome. But Paul's point, in context, is not that these distinctions of Jew and Greek, slave and free, male and female have ceased to exist. His point is that in Christ Jesus we believers are one, whoever we are. We all share a common relationship with him, and we are all equally "sons" of God.[8] The divisions have gone, but not the distinctions.

Moreover, as we shall see, there are (at least) two more problems with trying to use this Galatians text to reject biblical gender-based role distinctions, namely, that these distinctions predate the fall and that elsewhere Paul clearly urges different roles and responsibilities for redeemed men and women.

MAN AND WOMAN IN THE GARDEN

It is certainly true that in the fall, and ever since, men and women have been doing battle, as anyone with a moment's life experience can testify. But it is not true that the differences between man and woman started with the fall.

Not only did God create man as male and female in Genesis 1, but Genesis 2 tells us that he also created them in different ways, at different times, and for different roles, functions, and responsibilities (related to those different ways and times).

The man is the first focus of God's creative activity. He is first in the garden, and he alone receives God's command. He is "alone," and this is "not good." He names the creatures, thereby assigning them their place in creation, but still no helper fit for him is found. God makes the woman from a rib taken from the man and presents her to him.

She is a helper suitable for the man, so he sings with delight at meeting his *complement*—of the same substance but distinct and different from him, as the name he gives her suggests.[9] It is the man, too (not the man and woman together), who "shall leave his father and his mother" and cleave to his wife, initiating a new family (Gen. 2:24; Matt. 19:5; Mark 10:7).

In short, the man occupies a place in the narrative that the woman does not. It is not that he is more important or blessed or human than she is. It is that he has a temporal and relational priority. He is the first formed in God's creation (a fact of import noted in 1 Tim. 2:13). God forms him alone of dust from the ground (Gen. 2:7). She is made after him, and from him, and for him (1 Cor. 11:7–9) so that *together* they can fulfill the purposes for which God created them: to be fruitful and multiply and fill the earth and subdue it (Gen. 1:28). Without the woman, man cannot do this. Without the man, neither can she (cf. Gen. 3:20; 1 Cor. 11:11–12).

God gives them each other, and he gives them different roles and responsibilities. They are not the same; neither are their functions the same. He has responsibilities of authority and leadership arising from his temporal and relational priority, which are seen, for example, in his task of naming, in his receiving God's commands, and in his initiating a new family with the woman God brings to him. She is a helper fit for him, a description we will explore further shortly. There is order in their relationship, and their roles and responsibilities are not interchangeable.

These words can sound shocking to us. Perhaps only a few people think that gender is a social construct, but most of us—especially *women*—have learned to resist gender-based distinctions, and so this can make us quite uncomfortable, and in a sense it is understandable to have some unease.

All of us live this side of the fall, so none of us knows firsthand how wonderful that first relationship was! *Our* experience of male/female relationships, indeed of all relationships, has been tainted by sin—our own and others'. Even if we've been blessed with (relatively) happy lives, we know things can go wrong, and we often know it firsthand.

But it was not like that before the fall. There were no egos, power plays, manipulation, abuse, neglected spouses, workplace bullies, pornography, or sexist jokes. In fact, there were none of the experiences that make it hard for us to read this Genesis account and rejoice in God's good and perfect design for men and women.

However, another look at Genesis reveals things that might have escaped us on first reading, things that can help ease our unease.

The first is that Genesis 2 comes after Genesis 1. We have already been told that "man" as male and female is the pinnacle of God's creation. We know already then that there's no inferiority or superiority between the man and the woman. They are equal in the eyes and heart and purposes of God.

Second, notice what God is like. In Genesis 2, the name that appears, the LORD God, tells us he is a covenant-making God who is with his people and binds himself to them (Gen. 2:4; cf. Ex. 3:14–15).[10] He is in control, not the man. And he is the generous provider. He is on our side, and his original design for us is good, a blessing and not a curse.

Third, notice that creation is not complete without the woman. The man has a need, a lack he cannot fill. More than that, without her he is alone and it is "not good," the only deficit in God's good creation.

Fourth (and important for both men and women this side of the fall), the term "helper" (*ezer*) is not an insult or excuse for exploitation. To the contrary! It is a term most often applied to God as he helps his people.[11] It is also used for military force.[12] It is not a name for wimps, but neither does it mean the helper is stronger than the one being helped. It describes a type of relationship.

The point is that those needing help cannot do it on their own. So it is for the man. The woman is created for a relationship in which she is a helper fit for him—perfectly suitable. She is his opposite and complement.

There is an order in their relationship, an order based on function, not worth. As the first formed, the man has God-given responsibilities of leadership; as his helper, the woman has a God-given responsibility to accept the man's leadership; for example, she receives the name he gives her, she joins with him in the new family he creates, and she learns from him the command he received from God. She embraces her distinct role as a helper for him, and together they form a partnership of equals.

And, of course, all this is before Genesis 3 and the tragic and fatal events of the fall.

DISORDERING GOD'S ORDERLY CREATION

What happens in Genesis 3 then is not the cause or start date of gender roles but their rejection, disruption, and distortion. This is when paradise was lost and when the honeymoon ended.

In progressive steps, God's plan for relationships within his creation was rejected. Instead of the man and the woman ruling creation as his representatives under his rule, the Devil (in the form of a serpent)[13] led the woman, the woman led the man, and they each disobeyed the word of God. They rejected the goodness and truth of his command (Gen. 2:16–17) and tried to put themselves in his place. They also rejected their place in the relationships God had established, which is why the man is judged both for eating the fruit and for listening to his wife (Gen. 3:17).

Immediately, the easy and harmonious relationships within God's creation are lost—between creation and humanity, between the man and the woman, and with God. The only recourse for the man and the woman is to hide, from each other and from God.

Yet they cannot escape! Their Creator has become their judge, and he reasserts his original order, as he calls first to the man, "Where are you? . . . Who told you that you were naked? Have you eaten of the tree of which I commanded you not to eat?" (Gen. 3:9, 11; cf. 2:16–17).

But the man can't answer straight. He fesses up, but not before he has blamed the woman and the God who gave her to him: "The woman whom you gave to be with me, she gave me fruit of the tree, and I ate" (Gen. 3:12).

But God has not given up on them. Neither has he discarded his original pattern for relationships. However, every aspect of their existence will now involve struggle, showing the results of sin. Filling the earth and subduing it will be hard. Producing food and offspring will be hard. Instead of a joyous, ordered partnership of equals, the relationship of the man and the woman will now be a hard, disrupted partnership of equals (3:16). They are both fallen. Her willing help will instead be "desire" and his loving leadership will instead be "rule."

We get a sense of what these changes look like in the very next chapter, where the same words and similar sentence structure are applied to sin and Cain, when God tells Cain that sin's "*desire* is for you, but you must *rule* over it" (Gen. 4:7). There is a battle for control: sin desires to have Cain, but he must dominate sin. For the woman and her husband, this battle will arise from their respective self-interested responses of desire and rule. These post-fall distortions of God's original plan and purpose have played out in myriad expressions in all gendered relationships, especially marriage, ever since.

In fact, the Bible tells us that none of us and none of our relationships are as God intended them to be. But the wonderful news of the gospel is that in Christ each of us is a new creation (2 Cor. 5:17). When we trust in Christ, our sinful self is crucified with him, and by the work of his Spirit we are given new life and are being remade in his image—the image of Christ.[14] Both male and female, we are being renewed into the image of *true* humanity, the perfect image of the invisible God (2 Cor. 4:4; Col. 1:15). Our destiny is our perfection as true image bearers.

EVERYONE A NEW CREATION IN CHRIST

At this point it might seem as if we've taken the longest possible route to get to where we want to be, namely, a place where we can think biblically about ministry among women. It is as if all we wanted to do was drive from home to our local church, and instead we've circled the globe! But now that we have that big-picture view, we are in a better position to turn to our homes and our churches.

It is here that we come to the second further problem, noted earlier in reading Galatians 3:28 as overturning gender-based role differences; that is, the *same* author, the apostle Paul, elsewhere urges differing roles and responsibilities for men and women in marriage and in ministry. The apostle Peter does the same with marriage. It would be strange if Paul contradicted himself by saying one thing in Galatians and the opposite somewhere else. We might expect the Spirit-inspired, infallible Word of the sovereign God to speak with one voice. And, of course, it does.

There is no contradiction. As we shall see, these roles and responsibilities are about restoring us as image-bearing men and women and transforming us into the likeness of God through the renewing work of the Spirit.

Husbands and Wives Made New

We begin with the New Testament teaching about marriage, not because every one of us is or should be married and even less because marriage is the holy grail of human relationships. We start here because the gender-based differences to be lived out in the church—the household of God—are an expression of differences that are most intimately and exclusively seen in the relationship of husband and wife. We glimpse these differences in Paul's letter to the Colossians:

Wives, submit to your husbands, as is fitting in the Lord. Husbands, love your wives, and do not be harsh with them. (Col. 3:18–19)

Several things are evident in these two brief verses:

- Both wives and husbands are addressed directly as equal moral agents and individually held accountable for how they relate to their spouse.

- The responsibilities of wives and husbands are not identical or reversible or interchangeable: wives have one responsibility; husbands have another.

- There is an order in their relationship: one submits to the other, and one has authority of some kind (hence the instruction to husbands not to be harsh).

- These responsibilities are based not on personalities, incomes, intelligence, or social position. They are instructions to all wives and to all husbands.

- These responsibilities are not conditional or based on merit. Paul does not say, "*If* they do X, *then* submit or love," but "submit" and "love."

- The original language makes clear that the wife is to submit herself; that is, her submission is her considered and willing response. Her husband is not responsible to make it happen.

- The focus is on the husband's responsibilities and loving duty, not on his power or rights.

- Both responsibilities are countercultural: the wife's submission is not just "as is fitting" (i.e., culturally) but "as is fitting in the Lord," and husbands were usually not told to "love" their wives, especially with costly, forgiving Christlike love

(Col. 3:13–14). These are *Christian* responsibilities, not culturally based ones.

- These responsibilities reverse the post-fall distortions of Genesis 3:16, replacing her destructive "desire" and his harsh "rule" with willing submission and loving leadership, which were God's ideals from the start.

- Finally, neither response will come naturally to the sinful heart. This is why a wife's submission is to be "as is fitting in the Lord," and why Paul warns husbands not to be harsh. These responses belong to the new self that believers are to "put on," but only after they have "put off" the old self with its practices (Col. 3:9–10).

I hope you agree that this much is pretty clear. But this brief statement still leaves us with questions. How is the husband to love his wife? Why are husbands and wives to relate this way? Do these instructions imply inferiority and superiority? What if one party isn't a Christian? Does this really apply these days?

Fortunately, God hasn't left us in the dark. Several other passages in the New Testament also discuss the relationship of husbands and wives. They all teach this same ordered pattern in the marriage relationship, but they come at it from slightly different angles and so give us fuller understanding of what God intends (Eph. 5:21–33; Titus 2:5; 1 Pet. 3:1–7).

In Ephesians 5 we learn why the wife is to submit herself to her husband. It is because in God's purposes the husband is head of the wife, as Christ is the head of the church, and so as the church submits to Christ—in everything—so wives are to submit themselves to their husbands.[15] We also learn how the husband is to love his wife, and it is no light thing! He is to love his wife as Christ loved the church and gave himself up for her, and he is to love his wife even as he loves himself. He is to care for her, protect her, and lead her.

First Peter 3 tells us that this pattern of relationship holds even in marriages in which the husband is not a believer. But there's a twist. In those days, it was the husband who set the religious agenda for his household, and a wife ordinarily accepted his religion. But Peter is speaking to independently minded women who have rejected their husbands' religion and believed in Jesus, telling them to submit to their husbands (but not so that they disobey Christ), in the hope that their husbands might be won for Christ. Radical!

And in Titus 2, we see that the good conduct of wives and their submission to their husbands could have an even greater effect because the absence of these things would bring the Word of God into disrepute in wider society (vv. 3–5). Moreover, this was not the case just in the first century, because it was not first-century Cretan culture that was setting Paul's agenda; it was the purity and godliness that belong to Christ in all ages (2:11–14).

By the same token, the presence of instructions for slaves and masters in all these texts—and the welcome historical rejection of the institution of slavery[16]—is no indication that the instructions to husbands and wives were undesirable or culturally driven and therefore limited in their application for today. The New Testament writers treat slavery and marriage very differently. Marriage is consistently seen as a good thing that has its origins in the purposes of God in creation. Not so with slavery. No New Testament writer writes positively about it (except about our slavery to Christ). In fact, Paul urges slaves to take their freedom if it is at all possible. What the apostles do is regulate the practice of slavery.[17] They do not promote, endorse, or defend it. However, they certainly promote, endorse, and defend marriage and different roles within it.

If we were in any doubt about the enduring relevance of this biblical pattern for marriage, we'd only have to look again at Ephesians 5, because the pattern for human marriage is taken from nothing less than the perfect end-time marriage of Christ and his bride, the church. This marriage was planned before the foundation of the world, will last for all eternity, and transcends all times and cultures. This is the eternal model for all earthly marriages.

Of course, the analogy is not exact, even for Christian marriage, for within the ordered relationship of human marriage there is no inequality. In the perfect model, Christ is both Lord and Savior of his bride. In Christian marriage both husband and wife belong equally to the church, the body of which Christ is head, for which he died, and which he nurtures and cherishes (Eph. 5:23–32). Both equally are heirs of the grace of life (1 Pet. 3:7) and also members of "a people" who are God's own possession (Titus 2:14).

There is much, much more that could be said about these texts.[18] For our purposes it is enough to say that all these texts have the same message: there is an ordered relationship between a husband and wife, with corresponding roles and responsibilities that are not reversible or interchangeable. A wife is intelligently and willingly to submit herself to her husband, and a husband is sacrificially to love and lead his wife as her head and to protect, nurture, and care for her, as they are one flesh. They are each to serve the other, but they serve in different ways.

One Body with Many Parts

This brings us rather naturally to how these differences work out within the body of Christ. One of my favorite segments on *Sesame Street* is called "One of These Things (Is Not Like the Others)." It even has a catchy little song:

> One of these things is not like the others;
> One of these things just doesn't belong.
> Can you tell which thing is not like the others
> By the time I finish my song?

I mention this as we begin to consider the roles and responsibilities of women and men in church because it sums up the way we often think about things: if two things are different, then one of them doesn't belong. But on that reckoning no one would belong in the church, because the rather remarkable message of the New Testament is that in the church, by God's design, we are all different!

It should be clear by now that we share an awful lot when it comes to being part of Christ's church. We are all sinners saved by the same grace and all members of the same body. The same Spirit enables our membership and participation (cf. Acts 2:17–21). Yet despite these commonalities, there are differences that affect and determine our relationships and contributions.

We are given different gifts by the same Spirit.[19] There are different roles and functions to which we might be appointed.[20] There are differences in Christian maturity,[21] opportunity,[22] prominence and participation,[23] and age.[24] And there are gender differences.

The *Sesame Street* song could never be a Christian song unless the difference it was identifying—the *only* difference—was absence of faith in Christ.

With that in mind, let's consider three main texts that directly address the differences of men and women in the church of God. We will move from the most general to the most specific.

1 CORINTHIANS 11:2–16

The presenting issue in 1 Corinthians 11:2–16 is what men and women were doing with their heads while they were praying and prophesying in the regular worship gathering. Some of the men, it seems, were covering their heads, perhaps as a sign of spiritual one-upmanship. Some of the women were *un*covering theirs, perhaps as a sign of their new freedom in Christ, especially since it's likely their veils were a cultural symbol associated with gender and marriage.

By doing so, these men and women were blurring the distinctions between men and women and denying the order in their existing relationships.

But this was not acceptable. Men and women might be enabled by the same Spirit to pray and prophesy, but they are to do so as men and women, not as unisex, androgynous beings, and not by denying their relationships or the order within them. This is why Paul begins as he does (v. 3), by placing the relationship of men and women within the context of Christ as the head of every man and of God as the head of Christ. In other words, he sets the relationship of man and woman in the context of the ordered relations within the Godhead and in such a way that Christ shares a place with both men and women, as one *in* authority and one *under* authority.[25]

The issue, it turns out, was not the actual head coverings. It was that by doing what they were doing, these men and women were denying their God-ordained gender differences and relational order, which found its model in the relations of the Godhead. Theology, not culture, shapes Paul's teaching. Yet that theology was to be expressed in culturally meaningful ways. So while Paul believed both men and women should pray and prophesy, the cultural conventions that expressed gender and relational order were to be maintained even as they prayed and prophesied.

1 CORINTHIANS 14:26—40

When we flip forward to 1 Corinthians 14, these differences become even clearer. Paul again addresses the behavior of different parts of the gathered body of Christ. However, the issue is no longer what men and women were doing with their heads but ensuring that what happens when the church gathers actually benefits the whole church.

Two factors had to be balanced. There was the desire for everyone to participate and contribute. And there was the desire—in fact, the need—for everyone to learn and be built up in God's truth. The common good was the goal (12:7).

So tongues speaking was regulated. So was prophecy. In certain circumstances, both tongues speakers and potential prophets were to be silent (14:28, 30). In a similar vein, in some circumstances, women, too—probably wives, in particular—were also to be silent (14:34). But when?

Obviously, not all the time, for the expectation of these chapters (1 Corinthians 12–14) is that each member will have something to contribute, and Paul has just indicated that he expects women will be praying and prophesying (1 Cor. 11:5). So this is not a blanket ban on women speaking in church, just as the instructions to the other two groups weren't either!

Women were to be silent at a specific time: they were not to participate in weighing prophecies. Paul flagged this weighing activity back in 14:29 but went on first to regulate the potential prophesiers (men and women) before doubling back to identify who was to weigh what was prophesied, why that was so, and then to give some criteria for how prophecies were to be weighed (vv. 36–40).

It was during this activity that women were to be silent. Their willing nonparticipation was an expression of their submission. While both men and women could and were encouraged to speak in tongues, interpret, sing, pray, and prophesy, the authoritative task of governing and teaching the congregation through the evaluation and acceptance or rejection of prophecy was not a shared task. It was a responsibility of male leadership.

The reason for this was not cultural or situational. Paul points to "the Law," the written word of God, as the reason (1 Cor. 14:34; cf. 14:21). In all likelihood, he has in mind the first three chapters of Genesis, where the relationship of men and women is first established, as we have seen.

1 TIMOTHY 2:11—15

This brings us to the clearest and yet most controversial text on gender roles and functions in ministry: 1 Timothy 2:11–15. Like 1 Corinthians 14 this is cast in the negative, identifying something women weren't to do. In fact, there are two things a woman was not to do: she was not to teach, and she was not to exercise authority over men.

It is likely these two activities have some overlap, but they are not one thing. The same two activities are mentioned (with different words) in relation to overseers and elders (3:2, 4; 5:17) and also match with the two things women were to do: "learn" and "with all submissiveness."

Most of us have a sense of what exercising authority entails, but what sort of teaching were women not to do? Is it a blanket ban on any teaching by women in any context? No! In 1 Timothy and Paul's other letters, teaching is usually an authoritative activity of ongoing, intentional instruction in apostolic doctrine and Scripture. It is how God's people are instructed in God's truth, from God's Word, so that they hear—learn—his Word.[26]

So the teaching Paul has in mind is not all teaching—of piano, economics, or high school Christian education. His point is not even that women were never to teach God's Word. Paul's point is that women were not to deliver this sort of teaching to men.

When the household of God gathered to pray and worship and learn, women were not to teach in what we today might call "sermons" or "Bible talks," the formal, regular, authoritative instruction of God's people from his Word.

Why was that? It wasn't because of the quality of their teaching or that they could teach if they weren't teaching heresy or if they were properly trained. There's no indication that quality or heresy was the issue. Besides, why would Paul be happy to let women teachers loose on other women and children if this was the case?

There is no reason here to believe women can't be excellent teachers, and excellent Bible teachers, at that!

Neither was it because there was an *unless* clause; that is, women were not to teach men *unless* they only did it a few times a year, or *unless* they did it under the authority of the pastor or elders, or *unless* they were gifted to do so, or *unless* they felt called.

The reasons—the only reasons—are found in the next two verses (vv. 13–14). They are the temporal priority of the man (he was formed first) and the events of the fall (the woman was deceived, not the man). Once again Paul goes right back to God's purposes for man and woman in creation and what happened when those good purposes were rejected. Paul's instructions are not based on first-century Greco-Roman culture or localized problems. His reasons span human history and God's purposes for men and women. They, therefore, apply to us today. They are why the authoritative teaching, leadership, and discipline of God's household are responsibilities for men, and not just any men but suitably gifted and duly appointed men.[27]

So let's return to the *Sesame Street* song. It says that if something is different, then it can't belong. But it's not like this in the body of Christ, because in God's wisdom and kindness, there are many, many differences among us. We are all different, but we all belong.

And while the New Testament says that believers have a great many spiritual gifts and ministry opportunities in common and that we should be keen to see all these ministries flourish and to build Christ's church together, it also says that we are to do so in ways that reflect God's order.

Just as God's creation activity brought order from chaos, so now, as his household, we are to conduct ourselves in an orderly way and relate according to his order. Our relationships and contributions are to be shaped by gifting, function, role, age, and so on. In particular, there are some different ministry responsibilities between the genders in that certain roles and activities are for men and not for women; these are the related activities of authoritative teaching, doctrinal leadership, and the governing of God's people.

Moreover, both these things, the commonalities and the gender differences, find their origins in the first chapters of Genesis. We have a shared humanity as those made in the image of God and being remade in the image of Christ, and we are also made male and female, with different roles and responsibilities while we await the return of Christ. The New Testament also tells us that these differences reflect both the eternal marriage of Christ and the church and the asymmetrical divine relations within the eternal Godhead.

MINISTRY BY WOMEN

We are now in a position to consider ministry *by* women. We have seen there are a great many different gifts and ministries that women share with men. But what can often pass us by is how often we are given descriptions of women doing ministry in the New Testament.

There is the ministry of women in Christian communities. They played a role in the formation of assemblies[28] and acted as hostesses in homes where believers met.[29] They spoke in tongues, prayed, and prophesied,[30] and they demonstrated great industry and charity (Acts 9:36–41). Phoebe was a servant (lit. deacon) of the church and a patron, who probably gave financial, material, and administrative assistance (Rom. 16:1–2). Priscilla, and her husband, privately instructed Apollos (Acts 18:26). Widows showed hospitality, washed the saints' feet, and cared for the afflicted (1 Tim. 5:10). Women were "fellow workers" with Paul, presumably in the work of the gospel, and risked their lives for Christ.[31] Others traveled, labored, or were imprisoned.[32] Still others sent or received Christian greetings or received letters.[33]

There is the ministry of women as wives and mothers. Timothy's grandmother Lois and mother, Eunice, raised him to love the Lord and know the Scriptures (2 Tim. 1:5; 3:14–15). The worthy widows in Ephesus had been faithful to their husbands and raised their children well (1 Tim. 5:9). Paul even received motherly care from Rufus's mother (Rom. 16:13).

All over the New Testament there are women doing ministry, and that's before we even get to all those descriptions of Christians in general![34]

No less significant are the prescriptions, or instructions, about women involved in ministry. Two, in particular, come to mind.

The first concerns women who were deaconesses or the wives of deacons,[35] who were to be sound in doctrine and godly and faithful in lifestyle (1 Tim. 3:11). It is likely, as with male deacons, that their ministry involved practical care of those in the Christian community (cf. Acts 6:1–6), but their qualifications also suggest that their speech could either build or undermine faith and community, so it had to agree with God's Word.

The second concerns the task of the older women in Crete to teach what is good and so correct and train the younger women to love their husbands and children and to live upright lives (Titus 2:3–5). This text has its own chapter later in this book; but for now notice that Paul's instruction effectively meant that the older women were to take over the role of being mothers—spiritual mothers—to the younger women, who may or may not have been actual family. In other words, the relationships among the women were an expression of the familial bonds established in the gospel (cf. 1 Tim. 5:1–2).

There are more general comments about ministry by women: the contribution wives make to the godliness of their husbands through sexual intimacy (1 Cor. 7:1–5) and sharing Christ with them (1 Cor. 7:16; 1 Pet. 3:2); the need for women to care for widowed relatives (1 Tim. 5:16); and the greater freedom of unmarried women to serve Christ, compared to their married sisters (1 Cor. 7:8, 34, 40).

Finally, we can't forget Paul's command to all the Colossians, men and women:

> Let the word of Christ dwell in you richly, teaching and admonishing one another in all wisdom with psalms, hymns and spiritual songs, singing with thankfulness in your hearts to God. (Col. 3:16 AT)

That is, when we come together, everyone will participate and teach, encourage, rebuke, and admonish one another—women and men, young and old, whoever we are.[36] And we will all pray for the advance of the gospel and will all present the gospel to the world with our mouths and in our lives (Col. 4:2–6; 1 Pet. 2:11–12).

None of this should surprise us. Like our Christian brothers, we women are equipped for good works and ministry by the Spirit of Christ, and our mandate, with them, is to fill the earth with the message of Christ and present all people mature in him—women and men, boys and girls, in our families, inside and outside our churches, and throughout the world (Acts 1:8; Col. 1:28).

MINISTRY TO WOMEN

This brings us, finally, to the ministry *of* women *to* women, glimpsed already among the older and younger women in Crete and in a woman's ministry to widowed family members. We have seen that as women there are all sorts of ministries we can be involved in, but we are particularly well placed to minister to each other.

Of course, men can minister to women, and women can minister to men, even though those ministries will not be identical, and we may put certain provisions in place to ensure the propriety and safety of both parties (both women and men).

But it stands to reason that because men and women are different, biologically and relationally, women are better placed to know women, and men are better placed to know men, and so there is a particular benefit in women ministering to women, and men to men. There is the benefit of lived knowledge, and there is the rapport that exists between like and like.

I take it that this is partly what motivated Paul when he says he became different things to different people (1 Cor. 9:19–23). He recognized that it is easier to reach, win, and minister to people if you are like them. Gender-specific ministry is a case in point. Paul's example shows that you don't have to be a woman to minister to women—but it helps!

GROWING UP TO CHRIST WHO IS THE HEAD

There is a harvest field out there and a church family to which we belong, and God has enlisted and equipped us to serve and advance and defend the gospel in our homes, our churches, and our world— and we have been enlisted *as women*. Paul sums up well what that means for us (and our brothers):

> Speaking the truth in love, we are to grow up in every way into him who is the head, into Christ, from whom the whole body, joined and held together by every joint with which it is equipped, when each part is working properly, makes the body grow so that it builds itself up in love. (Eph. 4:15–16)

Whatever else you take away from this book, may it encourage you to grow up into Christ, who is the loving and only head of his true church, and to do everything possible to bring others to do the same.

— 3 —

The Word Passed On

Training New Leaders

Carrie Sandom

Who was the first person God used to teach you about the Lord, his death, and his resurrection? Maybe it was one of your parents, or a Sunday school teacher, or a friend at college or work. For me, it was my youth leader, a man called Harold Brown. I had been going to church with my sisters and grandparents for as long as I could remember and must have heard the gospel of Christ preached on numerous occasions. But it is Harold whom I specifically remember teaching me the gospel and how I needed to repent of my sins and put my trust in Christ's death. Soon after that, at a youth weekend away, the Lord graciously convicted me of sin and brought me to that point of surrender when I acknowledged Jesus as my Savior and my Lord. I don't know if Harold ever knew how significant his teaching was in that youth group, but I am hugely grateful for his

ministry and his faithfulness in proclaiming the gospel to a bunch
of unruly teenagers.

WHY TRAINING IS SO IMPORTANT

In 2 Timothy 2:2 Paul urges Timothy to be a faithful minister of the
gospel by passing on to future generations what he has been taught:

> What you have heard from me in the presence of many witnesses
> entrust to faithful men who will be able to teach others also.

There are four generations of gospel workers in that verse: *Paul*,
who taught it to *Timothy*, who had the responsibility of entrusting
it to *faithful men*, who in turn would teach *others*. The wider context demonstrates that this was Paul's ministry strategy in ensuring
that the gospel was guarded from false teachers and preserved for
future generations. The Pastoral Epistles (1 Timothy, 2 Timothy,
and Titus) all show that the appointing of faithful men as leaders
in the local church was a key component in this ministry strategy, but the principles outlined within these epistles can be applied
more broadly than that.[1] This is the way to guard the gospel in our
Sunday schools, youth groups, student campuses, women's Bible
studies, and senior fellowships: by entrusting it to faithful men and
women who in turn will be able to teach it to others. Two qualifications for the entrusted ones stand out in this verse.

1) They Must Be Faithful

It's no accident that Paul mentions the many witnesses present when
he taught Timothy. This was to remind Timothy that he was not at
liberty to change the message he received from Paul, and there were
plenty of people who could check that what Timothy passed on
was indeed the true gospel.[2] But Timothy also needed to be careful
that the men he entrusted with the gospel were also faithful and not

prone to changing the message. This was what the false teachers were prone to do and, sadly, often still do today. Timothy needed to teach the gospel faithfully and ensure that the men he trained up were able to do the same. They must be faithful. But that's not all.

2) They Must Be Able to Teach

This implies that not everyone is a gifted Bible teacher. Yes, we all have the responsibility of speaking about Christ. Both Peter and Paul made this very clear—calling us to be prepared, gently and respectfully, to make a defense to anyone who asks us for a reason for our hope (1 Pet. 3:15); and urging us, as the Word dwells in us, to teach and admonish one another (Col. 3:16). But some people are particularly gifted at teaching the Bible. And these were the people Timothy needed to entrust with the work of gospel ministry—men who were faithful in what they taught but also gifted in actually teaching it.

Both these qualities were needed. If these men were faithful but not able to teach, they would confuse their hearers. If they were able to teach but weren't faithful, they would lead them into heresy. Appointing faithful men and women who can teach others is not an easy task. We should be careful not to appoint the most knowledgeable people if they can't teach what they know; nor should we appoint the best communicators if they are not theologically reliable. This is why the Lord Jesus urges his disciples to "pray earnestly to the Lord of the harvest to send out laborers into his harvest" (Matt. 9:38).

It is a mark of the Lord's kindness that we have faithful men and women who are able to teach us the Bible today—but they are not innovators. They need to pass on what they have been taught by other faithful teachers, who in turn will have passed on what they were taught by others. The Lord Jesus has safeguarded the faithful preaching of the gospel in every generation from his earthly ministry until now, through his teaching and the commissioning of his apostles, through people like Timothy and other leaders of the early church, through the men that Timothy (and others) appointed to teach after them, and so on—all the way down to people like my youth leader, Harold.

This means that we have a tremendous responsibility not just to faithfully teach God's Word to others in our own generation but also to train up those who will be faithful teachers and trainers of the next generation of teachers and trainers. And in women's ministry it is no different. I am hugely grateful to God for the faithful men and women he has used to teach me the Bible and then to train me to teach and train other women to be teachers and trainers of others. But before we think about whom we should train and how we can train them, we first need to understand the bigger picture of God's plans and purposes.

HOW TRAINING FITS INTO GOD'S WIDER PLANS AND PURPOSES

There are three things that we need to understand: God's plan for the world, God's purpose for the church, and God's means for achieving this plan and purpose.

1) God's Plan for the World: To Unite All Things in Christ

According to Ephesians 1:9–10, God's "purpose, which he set forth in Christ as a plan for the fullness of time," is "to unite all things in him"—that is, under the lordship of Christ. This is the endgame to which all of history is heading—when, at the name of Jesus, every knee will bow, in heaven and on earth and under the earth, and every tongue will confess that Jesus Christ is Lord (Phil. 2:10–11). Knowing the end of God's plan, faithful ministers of God's Word will always have a heart for the lost, urging them to turn from their sins and acknowledge the lordship of Christ before he comes, at which time they will have no choice.

2) God's Purpose for the Church: To Be Rooted and Established in Christ

According to Colossians 2:6–7, God's purpose for the church is that we should be grounded in our faith, "rooted" and "established" in Christ, and forever thankful for all that he has done. The active metaphors of roots going down into Christ and being built up into Christ show that there is no room for complacency; there is always progress to be made. This means that faithful Bible teachers will encourage Christians to grow in their knowledge and love of Christ, to be rooted and established in him, and to be more and more thankful for all that he has done.

3) God's Means for Achieving This Plan and Purpose: Scripture

According to 2 Timothy 3:15–16, it is Scripture that makes us wise for salvation through faith in Christ, and it is Scripture that thoroughly equips us for ministry. All Scripture (both Old and New Testaments) is inspired by God and profitable for *teaching* and *reproof* (the Greek verbs imply the teaching of sound doctrine; in other words, what we believe); and also for *correction* and *training* in righteousness (the Greek verbs imply the practical outworking of ethical discipleship; in other words, how we behave). There is truth to be taught and error to be corrected. It is never enough just to teach the positives of Scripture; the faithful teacher of God's Word will also make clear the negatives.

WHOM TO TRAIN

But who is worthy of such a task? Well, at one level, none of us is. Paul affirmed that to be a teacher of God's Word is a noble task,[3] but James pointed out that it was not to be entered into lightly: "Not many of you should become teachers, my brothers, for you know that we who teach will be judged with greater strictness" (James 3:1).

The context shows that James is referring to the task of being an elder in the church, but, again, the principle can be applied more broadly. I take it that anyone who has a Bible teaching role—whether as a women's worker, or a student worker, or a Sunday school teacher—is in a position of great responsibility and influence.

So who is worthy of such a task? A couple of passages in the New Testament outline the criteria for appointing church leaders, but we'll look briefly at just one, from Paul's letter to Titus.[4]

> This is why I left you in Crete, so that you might put what remained into order, and appoint elders in every town as I directed you—if anyone is above reproach, the husband of one wife, and his children are believers and not open to the charge of debauchery or insubordination. For an overseer, as God's steward, must be above reproach. He must not be arrogant or quick-tempered or a drunkard or violent or greedy for gain, but hospitable, a lover of good, self-controlled, upright, holy, and disciplined. He must hold firm to the trustworthy word as taught, so that he may be able to give instruction in sound doctrine and also to rebuke those who contradict it. (Titus 1:5–9)

Paul had left Titus in Crete to appoint elders in every town. The criteria for appointing these men can be divided into three categories.

1) GODLY CHARACTER: TITUS 1:6—8

The elders needed to be well known and have a proven track record. They were to be above reproach in a variety of contexts. The Greek word means "blameless," not "unblemished." These men were not expected to be perfect (which, of course, would exclude everyone), but they were expected to be above reproach. The shift to the singular in verse 6 is significant: each man was to be considered individually.

The first context to be considered was the home. Each of these men needed to be a one-woman man and demonstrate a disciplined home life. He needed to lead and be in control of his own children (v. 6). The parallel passage in 1 Timothy makes the point that if a man is not able to manage his own family, then he won't be able to lead the family of God.[5]

The next area to be scrutinized was that of his relationships. He was not to be overbearing or arrogant or quick-tempered; he should not be a drunkard, or violent, or greedy (Titus 1:7); he needed to be kind and hospitable, someone who loved what was good; he needed to be disciplined and self-controlled in himself, upright in the eyes of others, and holy in the eyes of God (v. 8). In other words, he needed to be a man of integrity with a strong faith in Christ and trusting in Christ's righteousness alone.

2) FIRM CONVICTIONS: TITUS 1:9

The next criterion to be assessed was their doctrinal beliefs. These church leaders needed to hold firm convictions grounded in the Scriptures and in the apostolic teaching so that they were not easily swayed by the winds of false teaching that regularly plague the church. Titus needed to be sure that any prospective elder was known for his orthodox beliefs and able to hold firmly to what he had been taught (Titus 1:9).

The parallel passage in 1 Timothy goes even further and stipulates that church leaders were not to be recent converts, or they might become conceited and fall under the same judgment as the Devil.[6] This meant that the suitability of anyone for Bible teaching ministry needed to be assessed by others over a period of some time. The New Testament never encourages self-appointment. Even Timothy's suitability for ministry required time for Paul to assess.[7]

3) TEACHING COMPETENCE: TITUS 1:7, 9

The final criterion for appointing elders concerned competence to teach. Since elders were God's stewards and entrusted with God's work (Titus 1:7), they needed to be reliable communicators of God's truth, not just able to teach sound doctrine but also able to refute those who opposed it (v. 9). This confirms what we have seen: that it is never enough just to teach only what is true. People also need to know where they are going wrong so that their thinking and behavior stay on track.

Now, before we assume that these criteria don't apply to women because we're not in the category Scripture describes as "elders," let's see what Paul says about the teaching role he expected women to have and how Titus would know whom to select for this task. I think it's striking, in Titus 2:3–5, that pretty much the same three criteria are applied here to the older women, who have the task of teaching and training the younger women. I'm not sure that "older" in this passage necessarily refers to age, as we know that age, in and of itself, is no guarantee of maturity.[8] But Paul was clearly concerned that the women who were spiritually mature should teach and train the women who were younger in the faith, and the criteria for assessing their suitability are remarkably similar to those we have already seen.

1) Godly Character: Titus 2:3. The older women were to be reverent in the way they lived (Titus 2:3). Their love for the Lord Jesus and his Word needed to be evident, and their lives were to be lived for his glory alone. They were not to be slanderers or addicted to wine (v. 3). Much harm can be done to the reputation of the church and especially its leadership through the evil of slander, but the damage is often irreparable if the slanderers are drunk and out of control. The Cretans were known for their lies and their gluttony,[9] but Paul wanted these Christians—and specifically these women here—to live differently. Not that they were able to do this in their own strength. It was the grace of God that would enable them to say no to ungodliness and train them to live self-controlled, upright, and godly lives.[10] These older women needed to demonstrate godly character.

2) Firm Convictions: Titus 2:5. But the older women also needed to have firm convictions. Paul was concerned that the Word of God should not be maligned in any way. These women needed to be steeped in the Word of God, knowing what it taught, what it meant, and how it applied. Their lives needed to be shaped by the Word of God so that they were not open to the charge of hypocrisy. And they needed to hold firmly to the Word of God and not give in to pressure to change its meaning or make it more palatable. They needed to be able to say the hard things and not waiver in their convictions, even when they were opposed by others and unpopular for doing so. They were not to be like the women mentioned in Paul's second letter to Timothy—weak-willed women, loaded down with sins and easily led astray by passions and pleasures.[11] The older women in Crete needed to show that the Word of God was their passion and their final authority. They needed firm convictions.

3) Teaching Competence: Titus 2:3–4. And, lastly, older women needed to be competent to teach. Paul made clear that these women were needed to teach what was good, in other words, what was godly.[12] The Greek word for "teach" here does not imply a formal teaching position but a more informal teaching role. The complementarity of men and women in ministry undergirds this instruction. While Titus and the male elders had a formal teaching role, one that was to be exercised in the whole church, they nevertheless needed the older women to teach and train the younger women. This was a ministry that couldn't be undertaken by the eldership (because men cannot model godly womanhood to women!), and so they needed to rely on the spiritually mature women to do it for them, taking the younger women under their care and teaching them and training them to embrace their responsibilities as women of God.

The issues needing to be taught and modeled to the younger women are worthy of attention, although I'm sure this list is more illustrative than exhaustive. The younger women needed to be taught and trained (literally "brought to their senses") to love their husbands and children (v. 4). The word used for "love" is not the love of emotion and romance but rather of self-sacrificial service. They also needed to be taught about self-control and what purity looks like for women (v. 5). Both of these terms carry nuances of sexual fidelity and required single women to be celibate and married women to be faithful to their husbands.

Our twenty-first-century sensitivities may bridle at the thought of women having to work *at home* (v. 4), but we need to remember that in the first century, nobody went out to the office to work. The Cretans were also renowned for their laziness,[13] so one way these Christian women could shake off that reputation was by being *busy* at home (as the NIV puts it). Paul's emphasis here is not so much a stay-at-home stereotype for all women nor a prohibition of wives being professionally trained and having their own careers, but more a recognition that if a woman accepts the vocation of marriage and motherhood, then she has particular responsibilities to her husband and children. In all her work she will maintain a central commitment to her family—a commitment that must not be neglected.[14]

But godly relationships within the family are not the only ones mentioned here. The younger women are to be kind in all their relationships, both inside and outside the home. They are also to be subject to their *own* husbands. This means that good order in marriage and an understanding of a husband's headship role need to be taught, understood, and embraced. The submission in view is not that of all women to all men, but of each wife to her own husband. Note that Paul does not envisage husbands demanding submission from their wives; rather, he urges the wives to offer it voluntarily out of submission and reverence for Christ.[15] This is a significant distinction. The reason given for these instructions is also important: that the word of God may not be reviled. Here we have the first indication that godly living is a necessary part of our witness to the world (there are two more in 2:8 and 2:10). Paul is clear that Christian marriages and homes that demonstrate a combination of sexual equality and complementarity will beautifully adorn the gospel, but those who fall short of this ideal are in danger of bringing the gospel into disrepute.

We have looked at the criteria for selecting women to teach and train other women as well as some of the issues that need to be addressed. But what does this teaching and training look like in practice?

HOW ARE WE TO TRAIN NEW LEADERS?

Various contexts exist in which we can train leaders for Bible teaching ministry. But before discussing these contexts, let's consider a passage from Paul's first letter to the Thessalonians, where he reminds them of some of his discipleship methods. I encourage you to open your Bible and read 1 Thessalonians 2:1–12. Paul's strategy outlined in these verses has formed the backbone of many a leadership training course since then. Four things stand out in Paul's discipling of the fledgling Thessalonian church.

1) His Gospel Focus: 1 Thessalonians 2:2, 8–9

Paul never tired of declaring the gospel, the good news of Jesus Christ who died for our sins and rose from the dead. He brought the gospel to Thessalonica, even after suffering and being shamefully treated for preaching it in Philippi (1 Thess. 2:2). He shared the gospel with the Thessalonians and continued to preach it with boldness and winsomeness (v. 8); night and day he worked hard at his tent making so as not to be a burden while he proclaimed the gospel to them (v. 9).

This tells us that the gospel should not be neglected; on the contrary, it needs to be a central focus in our training. Yes, the gospel needs to be proclaimed to unbelievers, but we also need continually to teach it to ourselves, that we might be fully established in our faith and rooted in the Lord Jesus Christ. The gospel needs to be at the very heart of our leadership training. Do our trainees know it? Can they explain it? Are they living it out in practice? Do they understand that we are saved by grace and not by works? Do they know a gospel outline? Could they articulate the gospel in thirty seconds? Explain it in five minutes? Teach it in thirty minutes? If our leaders are to be faithful teachers of God's Word, they need to be able to teach the gospel. We must be gospel focused in our training.

2) His Transparent Life: 1 Thessalonians 2:1, 3, 5–6, 8–10

Paul was concerned to share not only the gospel with these Christians but also his whole life. Many people have observed over the years that the Christian life is both taught and *caught*. Jesus's own strategy was to focus on a few (the twelve disciples) and to share his life with them while he taught and trained them for future ministry. And here, the transparency of Paul's life was a major component in his own ministry strategy. The Thessalonians knew Paul well (1 Thess. 2:1). They knew about his suffering in Philippi and the ongoing opposition he faced whenever he preached the gospel (v. 3). His teaching did not spring from error or impure motives, nor was he trying to trick them (v. 3). He never sought to flatter them or take advantage of them, and he wasn't motivated by greed (v. 5). He didn't demand anything from them or seek glory for himself (v. 6). He shared everything with them (v. 8) and was careful to provide for his own needs (v. 9). His conduct amongst them was holy, righteous, and blameless (v. 10).

But all of this takes time! The Thessalonians would have come to know Paul in a variety of contexts, not just when he was teaching the Scriptures. They would have observed how he related to people, both believers and unbelievers; how he interacted with men and women, Jews and Gentiles, older people and young children. They would have seen the quality of his tent making, his interaction with other merchants and traders and the ruling authorities, and whether he paid his taxes. The transparency of Paul's life was evident. Here was a man who not only preached the gospel but also lived it out. The transforming power of the gospel in his own life had changed him from being a blasphemous persecutor of God's church to a faithful preacher and follower of God's Word.

This means that if we are the ones teaching and training others, we have got to let them know us. They need to see us outside of the study or the classroom; they need to see how we live, how we relate, how we spend our leisure time, what we joke about, and how we interact with people. We are not professional Christians; we are fellow servants of Christ and walk the same road—all of us. Our lives need to be transparent.

3) His Parental Concerns: 1 Thessalonians 2:7–8, 11–12

It is interesting to see how Paul describes his ministry to these young Christians. He has been like a mother and a father to them. When we read that he was gentle among them like a nursing mother taking care of her children (1 Thess. 2:7), we understand through this picture that he cared tenderly for their needs. I take it that Paul wasn't just delegating this kind of care to others but was intimately involved with the people in Thessalonica, and as a result they were very dear to him (v. 8).

But he was also like a father to them. He develops this picture by explaining that he exhorted them, personally and individually;

he encouraged them and urged them to live lives worthy of God (vv. 11–12). The words for *exhort, encourage,* and *urge* are all teaching words implying the need for both careful instruction and urgent rebuke. Paul would not have left things unsaid that needed to be said. His fatherly love for these Christians would have included both encouragement and rebuke when needed, as he longed for the gospel to bear fruit in their lives.[16]

In our training of leaders we need to demonstrate and recommend the same parental concern as Paul, showing gentleness and care for each person but also urgency in our teaching that doesn't allow ungodly behavior to go unchallenged. I suspect we all find this difficult—some of us because we are too gentle and find it hard to say the tough things, and others because we are too focused on the given task to know when to show gentleness and compassion. The Lord Jesus perfectly modeled both of these qualities; we need to pray for his wisdom as we teach and train others.

4) His Integrity before God: 1 Thessalonians 2:4, 5, 10

Paul never abused his leadership role, and he was conscious that one day he would give an account of how he had conducted himself before God. He knew that God would test his heart (1 Thess. 2:4) and twice calls God to be a witness—first of all, to his not being motivated by greed (v. 5) and then to his righteous conduct among them (v. 10). Paul is not claiming perfection here, but he is blameless of any charge that might be brought against him. He was a faithful minister of the gospel and lived it out in practice, trusting in the atoning blood and righteousness of Christ that meant he was no longer condemned.[17]

This is a challenge to our own integrity before God, who knows our hearts, an integrity that does not rely on our knowledge of the Scriptures, or our teaching ability, or the reputation we may have, but depends solely on Christ and his work of grace in our lives. To be faithful ministers of the gospel we need to know how totally dependent we are upon his grace. We dare not—indeed, we cannot—teach or train others without this.

WHAT TO TEACH AND WHERE TO TRAIN

We have looked at why training is so important as a ministry strategy in the local church, how training people to teach the Bible fits into God's overall plans and purposes for the world, whom to train as leaders, and some of the methods Paul himself used. Finally, let's consider what content people need to be taught and in what contexts they should be trained. There are various training contexts. Below are four that I have been involved with over the years.

1) Training for One-to-One Ministry

If training women for Word ministry is a new concept for you, and rather a daunting one at that, this is the best place to start. It is also the easiest to fit into a busy schedule. In all the churches in which I have worked, I have sought out mature Christian women who love the Lord and are hungry for his Word. They may shy away from the thought of formal training and may not have had any experience of being taught by women in the past or how crucial it is for the life of the local church. It doesn't matter, at least not to start with. These things develop over time.

All you need for one-to-one leadership training is a Bible, a cup of tea, and a commitment to meet regularly for about an hour and a half! I've done one-to-one's in coffee shops, but I prefer to meet in my own home where there are fewer distractions and where I can determine when to bring things to a close. In a typical session I would aim to use the time as follows:

- Tea/coffee and general catch-up: 15 minutes.
- Bible study and praying through the passage: 45 minutes.

- Talking and praying through related issues and concerns: 30 minutes.

The catch-up at the start is crucial. We need to share our lives and so find out about each other's families, who we're concerned about and how to pray for them, where our Christian witness is most challenging (at home, college, or work), and for whom we are praying for opportunities to witness. These can then be prayed about later in the session.

The Bible study needs to be directed but informal. The dynamic is different when there are only two people. I try not to have lots of questions written out on large pieces of paper (which can demoralize the other person), but just a small card inside my Bible with a few notes—either questions to ask or points from the passage that I want us to talk about. The aim is not to teach them everything there is to be learned from the passage (which will exhaust them), but to talk about a few things from the passage—what those things mean (not just what they say) and how they apply today.

At one level, it really doesn't matter what book of the Bible you study. All of God's Word is profitable for teaching, rebuking, correcting, and training in righteousness. Nevertheless, I think it's good to aim at manageable chunks of Scripture in one-to-one study. In the past I have studied Genesis 1–3 (foundational for understanding who God is and what it means to be made in his image); Ephesians (for clarity about salvation and living as God's redeemed people); 2 Timothy (full of practical ministry principles); and Titus (enlightening about women-to-women ministry in the local church).

To close, we always *pray in* what we have learned from the passage and then let the conversation move onto other related issues (pastoral issues that have emerged since we last met, a sermon we may have been particularly challenged by, and so forth). After meeting for six months to a year, my aim is always to encourage them to meet up with someone else and pass on what they have learned, which then frees me to meet with someone else. If this model of training goes well, then, at the end of the second year, there will be four of us ready to meet up with four others. By the end of five years you will have raised up quite a significant number of women who are able to teach and train others. It really is that simple!

Resources worth checking out for training people in one-to-one ministry include:

- Sophie Peace, *One to One: A Discipleship Handbook* (Milton Keynes, UK: Authentic Lifestyle, 2003)

- David Helm, *One to One Bible Reading* (Sydney, AU: Matthias Media, 2012)

- Andrew Cornes, *One 2 One: Bible Studies for Bible Reading Partnerships* (Purcellville, VA: Good Book Company, 2003)

- Phillip Jensen and Tony Payne, *Just for Starters: Seven Foundational Bible Studies*, rev. ed (Sydney, AU: Matthias Media, 2003)

2) Training Bible Study Leaders in the Local Church

This next context—the training of small-group leaders—is really no different. The best way is always to teach the Bible to them first and then encourage them to teach it to others. Over the years I have regularly met with the leaders of various women's Bible study groups (whether students, professionals, stay-at-home moms, those who work part-time, or the retired—or any mixture of the above) and studied a Bible passage with them a week ahead of the time they will study it with their own groups. In addition I have run various training workshops where we have looked at the different biblical genres and seen what tools are needed to get to the heart of each.[18] I have also run sessions that cover much of the content of this chapter. My aim is always to teach the Bible first of all, and then to see how the biblical principles can be applied to our own particular church context. The Pastoral Epistles are a rich treasure trove of ministry principles for Bible teachers, so, in a five-year cycle, I aim to teach them at least once.

In addition, there are various other components to incorporate into a leadership training program, either with material I have written myself (the advantage being that I can tailor it to the women I seek to train) or with material published by others. I'll mention two examples of other important components.

First, *a Bible overview*, looking at the big picture of God's redemptive purposes from creation to new creation. Faithful Bible teachers need to know how the Bible fits together and what covenantal promises God has made to his people at various points in history—Abraham, Moses, David, during and after the Babylonian exile—and how those promises are fulfilled in Christ. An understanding of the different types of biblical genres is also important: How is studying Judges or the Psalms different from studying Colossians or Revelation? Some of the resources available include:

- Christopher Ash, *Remaking a Broken World: The Heart of the Bible Story* (Milton Keynes, UK: Authentic Media, 2010)

- Vaughan Roberts, *God's Big Picture: Tracing the Storyline of the Bible* (Downers Grove, IL: InterVarsity, 2003)

- Phil Campbell and Bryson Smith, *Full of Promise: Understanding the Old Testament* (Sydney, AU: St. Matthias, 1997)

- Carrie Sandom, *Bible Toolkit #1: The Story of the Bible (Creation to New Creation)*, http://thegospelcoalition.org/2014

Second, an *evangelism training* course: learning how to share the good news clearly and effectively. *Two Ways to Live* is one excellent resource for training people in the gospel.[19] Not only does it give a useful gospel outline to learn (with six pictures for visual learners and six accompanying Bible verses), but it also teaches a basic systematic theology, covering the doctrines of creation, sin and God's wrath, the cross, the resurrection, and final judgment. These clear points prepare people to answer the questions and objections often raised by enquirers, such as:

- Hasn't science disproved Christianity?
- Why do good people go to hell?
- Wasn't Jesus just a good moral teacher?
- Is Christianity just one of many ways to God?
- What evidence is there for the resurrection?
- How can a God of love allow so much suffering in the world?
- Can't I leave it until I'm retired and have more time to think about it?

In addition, there are numerous basic online courses available through various institutions and organizations that can help equip people for Word ministry.[20] It can be extremely helpful for a group of church leaders and/or potential leaders to work together through a well-developed series of courses in order to build an integrated, cohesive, and internally consistent understanding of the Bible and Christian doctrine.

3) Mixed-Mode Leadership Training with Part-Time Study and Ministry Placements in the Local Church

Over the last twenty years in the UK, a growing number of *regional ministry training courses* have been established that offer the option of what we call "mixed-mode training." To explain this third training context I will describe some of the training ministries with which I have been involved, not to prescribe them as the only possible options but in order to encourage growing consideration of possible avenues of training in the church at large.

The trainees (men and women) in these regional courses are

often recent university graduates in their early twenties (but not exclusively, as some churches prefer them to have more experience) who have a ministry placement in a local church for one or maybe two years. They attend the training course one day a week and work the rest of the week in their churches, doing a range of practical and administrative tasks as well as some real-life Bible teaching—whether in the children's ministry, youth ministry, women's ministry, or men's ministry—under the supervision of a more experienced Bible teacher.

Based on the Ministry Training Scheme established in the 1980s by Phillip Jensen at St. Matthias Church, Sydney, the regional training courses offer a two-year program involving one class day per week, usually four intensive sessions per day: *Bible Exposition*; *Biblical* and then *Systematic Theology*; *Ministry Question Time* (in which questions from trainees on doctrinal or pastoral issues arising from their church work are answered by a panel of experienced Bible teachers); and *Bible Teaching Workshops* (in which trainees teach the Bible to each other in small groups and then receive feedback, led by an experienced Bible teacher).

The *Cornhill Training Course* is another mixed-mode training course, one that runs two days weekly over two years.[21] Part of the ministry of the Proclamation Trust in London, Cornhill was established in 1991 by two clergymen with a passion for biblical exposition, David Jackman and Dick Lucas. Each student at Cornhill is encouraged to have a Word-ministry focus in his or her church, where most would be working during the rest of the week under the supervision of an experienced Bible teacher.

The course offers training in expository Bible teaching, with a particular emphasis on equipping men to preach while also preparing women and men for other Bible-teaching ministries. The heartbeat of the course is the expository teaching of a wide range of Bible books. Tools for unpacking the seven different biblical genres are taught in order to develop good exegetical skills. This basic Bible-handling program is complemented by foundational teaching on prayer and the heart; principles of exposition; biblical theology; and systematic theology.

The Women's Ministry Stream became an integral part of the Cornhill syllabus in 2000, developed as a result of a growing concern that while Reformed evangelicals agree that men and women have different roles to play in the life of the local church, many ministry training schemes (and theological seminaries) train them as if they don't. The Women's Ministry Stream sought to correct this by specifically equipping women for the types of Bible teaching ministries in which they are likely to be involved—whether full-time or part-time, paid or unpaid, members of church staff teams or not.[22] The courses in Cornhill's Women's Ministry Stream run for roughly one day a week in the second year and include: *Biblical Womanhood*; *Ministry Issues*; *Pastoral Issues*; and *Bible Teaching Practice Classes*.

The advantage of these mixed-mode training courses is that they keep students rooted in the local church, where they have opportunity to put what they're learning into practice while they are still learning it! Being supervised by an experienced Bible teacher is also an important component and, where this works well, the training, accountability, and encouragement often continue long after the ministry apprenticeship has finished.

4) Full-Time Theological Training in Seminaries and Bible Colleges

Not everyone will have the opportunity to study full-time at a theological college or seminary, but women should at least consider it. It can be costly both in time and money, but, increasingly, scholarships are available.

There are various considerations. For example, the type of

seminary is important (Is it denominational, university-based, or independent?), and the type of courses and degrees offered is obviously key. But most crucially it is important to consider the faculty: Do they revere the Word of God? Are they committed to teaching the Bible or just talking about the Bible? Do they teach a solid, coherent biblical theology, one that is committed to the gospel of Christ, to penal substitution as the means of our atonement, to the sovereignty of God in all things, to the evangelization of the world through the preaching of the gospel, to the transforming power of the Spirit, and to the importance of good order in the local church? If these are all affirmed, then it should be a good place to study. Of course, the Lord will lead some to study in academic institutions where all these things are not affirmed or not univocally affirmed, and then it will be a matter of doing what each of us must indeed always do: keep searching the Scriptures faithfully, seek out wise and trusted counsel along the way, and stay well enfolded in a strong, biblically based local church.

I advise women not simply to send off an application without first talking it through with a pastor and other Christian friends—those who know you well and will tell you truthfully if this might not be a good investment of your gifts. If you don't enjoy academic study, then seminary might not be the place for you; if you have teaching gifts but no heart for ministry, then it probably won't be the place for you, either. But if you have the heart, the opportunity, and the gifting—then go for it! It's sometimes hard for women to know exactly how the Lord will use their theological training. You might become a faculty member yourself and teach other students; you might go into business and lead your colleague to Christ after months of talking over a coffee after work; you might be involved in training women in your local church; or you might use it to teach your children at home. One thing is for sure: wherever you use your seminary training in the future, it will never be wasted.

No biblical training is wasted in God's good economy. It is a privilege to invest ourselves in the training of women who will be able to help pass on the good news in all the diverse contexts of their lives. It is a delight, this training, as we see strong, godly women growing up in the church and bearing witness to God's gospel truth. It is a necessity, this training, so that one generation will with full voice keep declaring God's grace in Jesus Christ to the next.

PART 2

CONTEXTS
FOR WOMEN'S
MINISTRY

— 4 —

The Local Church

Finding Where We Fit

Cindy Cochrum

Nayana first walked through the doors of our church when she was invited by a friend to attend our women's Bible study.[1] Having lived most of her life in a predominantly Muslim country, she was curious about the Bible. Curious, but also skeptical.

The small-group leaders who welcomed her were eager to share the truths of God's Word with her. They invited her into their homes for meals and spent time outside of the study answering her questions about Jesus. Nayana was convinced that Jesus was a good man. She believed he was one in a line of prophets but not the Son of God.

Week after week Nayana attended our Bible study. She participated in the small-group discussions, passionately defending and even promoting her Islamic faith. She often remained after the lecture time to ask questions of the teachers. Language and cultural barriers made it difficult for us to read her intentions.

Our women's leadership team prayed for Nayana's salvation, for her small-group leaders, and for the Lord's guidance of the other women involved in the study. We sought advice from our pastoral leadership. Nothing seemed to change.

But God by his Spirit was quietly using his Word to soften Nayana's heart and open her eyes. After nearly a year of studying the Bible, Nayana put her faith in the Lord Jesus Christ.

There was no question about the authenticity of her conversion. The hardness that had once characterized her comments began to soften. Nayana's questions took on a note of sincerity. Her eyes danced as she spoke of Jesus as her Lord and Savior. She became involved in the activities of the church, regularly attending our Sunday services. She was hungry to learn more and took advantage of every opportunity to hear God's Word taught. She was quickly integrated into the life of the church.

But Nayana's growing commitment to the Lord was costly. Her husband was opposed to the change he saw in Nayana's life. He demanded that she stop attending Bible study. He confiscated her phone to keep her from communicating with anyone involved. Eventually he left her with their two sons, no income, and overwhelming debt. Her extended family threatened her life. Her sons questioned her Christian faith. But within the body of Christ, Nayana discovered a deeper bond than she had ever known. New brothers and sisters in Christ welcomed her and her sons into their homes for meals. They spent hours answering questions and teaching her about what it means to follow Jesus. The church helped with her financial needs and with maintenance of her home.

Within a few years, Nayana's sons began to attend our Sunday morning worship services. They had witnessed Nayana's transformation and found themselves curious about Christianity. As they heard God's Word preached and met God's people, the Holy Spirit began to work in their lives as well. Both of her sons also gave their lives to the Lord.

Now, several years later, Nayana's sons have moved away for schooling, but she remains a vibrant part of our local church. Her eyes continue to shine as she talks of the Lord and his care for her. She recently invited other women to join us in our study—women whose lives are strikingly similar to hers when we first met.

Nayana's story is beautiful because it is the story of new life and redemption through Jesus. It's also beautiful because it's such a clear picture of the body of Christ at work. We certainly didn't do our part perfectly. There were lessons for us to learn at nearly every step along the way—lessons about cultural barriers, about sensitivity, about the power of God's Word, and about trusting him. But the Lord was at work through his church, drawing Nayana to himself, strengthening his people, and ultimately accomplishing his purposes in spite of our failings.

As he wrote Nayana's story, the Lord used the strong connection between our women's Bible study group and the local church of which we are a part. This connection allowed Nayana to experience the strength and beauty of the entire body of Christ. Nayana was drawn most immediately to the women and the relationships that she developed around God's Word in Bible study. She would not have been comfortable attending a mixed group as a first step. The whole church body, however, provided guidance, support, and prayerful encouragement as our leadership team prayed for direction and ministered to this seeking woman. After Nayana came to know the Lord, the church came alongside her to help with practical, concrete needs. Eventually, she and her sons were integrated into the body of Christ. Now she is inviting her friends to join us in our women's Bible study.

LIFE IN THE EARLY CHURCH

Stories like Nayana's must have been common in the early church. In the book of Acts, which tells about the founding of the church, starting in Jerusalem and moving outward, Luke describes an increasingly diverse community that included people from various countries, speaking different languages but drawn together by their common faith in Jesus Christ. Some of those early meetings must have been breathtaking, offering a mosaic of different skin colors, clothes, hairstyles, and languages—a sea of new believers joining together in praise and worship.

As the good news of salvation through Jesus spread, local church groups began to spring up in surrounding cities. As time went on, challenges arose among the various communities of believers. Letters like those of the apostle Paul and the apostle Peter offer us glimpses into some of the difficulties that the various early churches faced.

The church in Corinth offers one example of the challenges that arose as God's people began to live life in community, under the authority of God's Word. Before we jump into a more practical discussion of what women's ministry looks like in the context of today's church, it is helpful to establish that context biblically.

When Paul first arrived in Corinth to share the message of the gospel, he found a city teeming with energy. This metropolis was a center for intellectual life and a crossroads for trade. People from various cultures and backgrounds regularly traveled through their busy city.

A year and a half later, when Paul left Corinth, a new church had been established. The community was young and alive. Welcoming new believers was a regular part of their lives. But it wasn't long before challenges began to arise.

Paul was concerned as he sat down a few years later and penned his letter to the Corinthian believers. Word of divisions within their community had reached Paul, and the church leaders had written to him asking for help. Pressures of a pagan culture pressed in from outside the church, and the challenges of dealing with real people (i.e., real sinners!) began to develop inside the church. Tiny fault lines were beginning to grow as believers pursued their own agendas. Divisions were forming as people began to follow and identify with various leaders. Some claimed to be loyal to Paul. Others followed Apollos or identified with Cephas. And those who wanted to trump everyone else claimed only to follow Christ. This was a dangerous situation. The schisms within the church threatened to derail the faith of the believers and undermine the work of Christ in Corinth. In an effort to counter these divisions, Paul opens his letter with a reminder of their common identity:

> To the church of God that is in Corinth, to those sanctified in Christ Jesus, called to be saints together with all those who in every place call upon the name of our Lord Jesus Christ, both their Lord and ours. (1 Cor. 1:2)

Paul emphasizes the common bond among the believers who make up the church in Corinth. They are all part of "the church of God": their community belongs to him. They are "sanctified in Christ Jesus": their position before God is solely determined by the work of Jesus on the cross on their behalf. And they are "called to be saints together"—called to a community of lives transformed by the power of the risen Christ.

The reality of the gospel was the essential grounding for all of life in their community. These brothers and sisters were united through the grace and mercy of Jesus. Paul leaves no room for pride or individualism. Every word in his letter flows directly from the truth of the gospel. That truth would serve as the foundation for Paul's blueprint for ministry.

In his letter, Paul addresses a host of questions about life in the local church, each one inextricably linked to the health and effectiveness of their ministry as a body of believers. He gives directions regarding how to navigate the challenges of sexual immorality and lawsuits among them. He provides instructions to the young church, teaching them about marriage, about celebrating communion, and about the resurrection.

In chapters 12–14 Paul addresses the question of spiritual gifts, bookending these chapters with the purpose for which the various gifts are given: "To each is given the manifestation of the Spirit for the common good" (1 Cor. 12:7). And then in 1 Corinthians 14:26b: "Let all things be done for building up." The point is clear: individual gifts are given *for the common good* and to be used *for building up* the local church. God has equipped each person by providing through his Spirit a specifically designed set of gifts, perfectly suited to serve the local church in Corinth, for the glory of Christ.

So, what happened in Corinth? As members unselfishly used their gifts to build up the church, the church became a picture of Christ to the world around them. God's Word was proclaimed with power, worship services were organized and well run, and challenging questions were handled with wisdom. Sexual purity was lived out and honored. Needs were eagerly met, and relationships were strengthened around meals in various homes—*no*, this is not what happened. This is what would have happened if the Corinthian believers had indeed used their gifts for the common good to build up the church.

Here's what actually happened: as various members of this congregation became discontent with their roles, divisions began to form. Some were proud of their gifting and began to think that their roles were the key to the success of the local church. They began to devalue the gifts of others—forgetting that "there are varieties of gifts, but the same Spirit" (1 Cor. 12:4). Rather than grounding their identity in Christ, many began to attach themselves to one important leader or another. Some began to look to those outside of their congregation for affirmation and teaching. The surrounding pagan world exerted its influence, and sinful behavior was tolerated. All of this threatened the ministry of the church in Corinth.

What picture could Paul use to communicate the reality of the Corinthian believers' position in Christ and their need for one another? What better analogy than that of a healthy, well-functioning human body?

> For the body does not consist of one member but of many. If the foot should say, "Because I am not a hand, I do not belong to the body," that would not make it any less a part of the body. And if the ear should say, "Because I am not an eye, I do not belong to the body," that would not make it any less a part of the body. If the whole body were an eye, where would be the sense of hearing? If the whole body were an ear, where would be the sense of smell? But as it is, God arranged the members in the body, each one of them, as he chose. If all were a single member, where would the body be? As it is, there are many parts, yet one body. (1 Cor. 12:14–20)

What an amazing picture of both diversity and unity! Every member of the Corinthian church had a vital role to play in the health of the church. Every follower of Jesus has received gifts through the Spirit. No exceptions. That means no one is off the hook, and no one is in a class of uber-elites.

When the Corinthian church was functioning well—with its members valuing one another and working together for the good of Christ's church—this young community of believers would serve as a powerful reflection of the grace, love, and mercy of Jesus to the watching world in Corinth.

IMPLICATIONS FOR TODAY

Paul's analogy reaches across the centuries into our own world. Like the Corinthian believers, we have been called to live in community with our brothers and sisters in Christ. We face challenges quite similar to those of the young Corinthian church in our twenty-first-century context.

It is often a messy business to live week in and week out with brothers and sisters in the church, fellow sinners who are growing in their love for Jesus and for each other. It can be tempting to avoid the more complicated connections that involve time in the physical presence of needy people. Our world overflows with theological books, expert online sermons, and bloggers who blog with widely celebrated authority. We can easily begin to idealize and identify with virtual voices and leaders, as opposed to real live and really imperfect ones. It's easier to jump online than to get ourselves (and perhaps others as well) ready and make our way to a church gathering, especially after a long day or week of work of whatever kind.

When our most important communities become something other than the church body in which the Lord has placed us, we miss out on the joy that comes from actually living in fellowship with the very people whom the Lord has gifted us to serve. The type of community that Paul envisions cannot occur in online chat rooms, forums, or in the comments section at the bottom of a blog; it requires loving and caring followers of Christ who are consistently and personally in touch with one another's lives. It requires members of a healthy and connected body working together for the same purpose.

Engaging in the local church brings much more joy and far more challenge than interaction through technology. We can't always choose our own timing in responding to requests. We don't have the option of simply "unfollowing" or "unfriending" someone. That difficult person will likely be sitting in the same place next week—at our next worship service. He or she will probably continue to make the same kinds of irritating comments or to sing too loudly or to keep missing the point in conversations or to do a host of other things that drive us crazy. This is what John Stott describes as the "paradox of the local church":

> It is the painful tension between what the church claims to be and what it seems to be; between the divine ideal and the human reality; between romantic talk about "the bride of Christ" and the very unromantic, ugly, unholy, and quarrelsome Christian community we know ourselves to be. It is the tension between our final, glorious destiny in heaven and our present, very inglorious performance on earth. This is the ambiguity of the church.[2]

Isn't this the reality that we believers all face? In Christ, the church is a beautiful community of brothers and sisters. But our daily experiences remind us of our fallen state and our need for a Savior. Every woman who has spent time investing in her community of believers has experienced this "painful tension." But as recipients of God's love and grace, we are gifted and called to engage in the life of the church and specifically of our local church, among his flesh-and-blood people. This kind of investment will bring glory to God and joy to us as we use the various gifts God has given us in the context for which they were given.

All of us have carefully and intentionally chosen a gift for someone we love. We wrap the gift in beautiful paper, present it to the recipient, and then watch with anticipation as it is opened. How will our loved one respond? Will he or she like it? Will it be clear just why we gave this exact gift and how well it fits the person and his or her personality? But how do we feel if, after opening the gift, the person sets it aside or uses it for some purpose other than the reason it was given?

Spiritual gifts are infinitely more valuable than human gifts. These precious, flawlessly distributed gifts are to be used in community, through the power of the Spirit who gives them, to build up our brothers and sisters and to grow the church as a light shining in a dark world. The gifts of the Spirit are perfectly suited to the individuals who receive them. They are also perfectly suited to meet the needs of the body of Christ and are distributed in an amazingly balanced way among congregants of a local church.

But just like the people in Corinth, we can be tempted to misuse our gifts, perhaps by overestimating them, perhaps by neglecting them, or perhaps by investing them in ways that do not build up the church—maybe even by simply deciding to use our gifts only elsewhere. In reality, the world outside the church often offers higher paychecks and much greater recognition.

When the gifts of any part of a church are misused or not used, the local body of Christ is left with a void. We've all experienced this reality in our physical bodies. If one part of our body isn't working well, other parts are forced to overcompensate and eventually become exhausted. Sometimes the contributions of missing members of the church cannot be replaced—the absence simply means vital roles will not be filled.

The community Paul envisions as he writes to the Corinthians is filled with people who are willing to step up and get involved in the day-to-day issues that come from living life in community, people who routinely ask questions like: "How and where can I serve most effectively?" "What responsibility has the Lord put in front of me?" "What needs do I see that I could fill today?" Ministry among women thrives as women employ their various gifts in this way. Some will be gifted as teachers, for example, others as evangelists, some as administrators or leaders of ministries, and still others as agents of mercy, generosity, and service to those in need (see Rom. 12:3–8).

In chapter 9 you will read about churches in India and South Africa where the men are largely absent, leaving a huge void. In some churches in the United States, the middle-aged women seem to be disappearing, withdrawing from active involvement in the life of the church. Many are finishing their child-rearing years and moving on to other kinds of work and involvement, leaving behind involvement with the church. What a difference it could make if such segments of the church population were both alive in Christ and vitally connected to his body.

Investment in the local church requires humility. Once again, we find our own reflections in the words to the Corinthian believers. Those with more visible gifts can be tempted to think of themselves in a special class that is more valuable than others (1 Cor. 12:24b–25). Jesus gives his church diverse and precious gifts for one purpose: to strengthen his church, through which he will make himself known to the world. It's all for his glory—not ours.

Aiming to encourage the proper and full use of women's gifts, we can easily slip into an effort to raise the status or increase the self-importance of women. What we're after can become slightly adjusted, as the goal of strengthening women somehow separates itself from the goal of strengthening the church. In his commentary on 1 Corinthians, Charles Hodge notes:

> When God's gifts, natural or supernatural, are perverted as a means of self-exaltation or aggrandizement, it is a sin against their giver as well as against those for whose benefit they were intended.[3]

Ministry among women is not a stepping stone to increased equality or a bridge to expanded opportunity. Various kinds of gifts are given to believers for the purpose of building up our brothers and sisters. When we remember the undeserved grace and mercy that we have been shown at the cross, we find it easier to keep our focus on Jesus and the beauty of the gospel rather than on ourselves. This is what it looks like to use our gifts "for the common good."

WHERE DO WE FIT IN THE CONTEXT OF OUR LOCAL CHURCH?

As women, finding our spot in the local church can be challenging. While every gift is equally valuable within the body, God's gifting of women extends far beyond changing diapers and making coffee. No one of us in the body should ever despise these tasks. Neither should we forget to look among women for a great diversity of gifts, perspectives, wisdom, and experience.

In chapter 2, Claire Smith addresses the boundaries that the Lord has established. Scripture is clear that the roles of ordained pastor and elder are reserved for our qualified brothers in Christ. Seeking to fill roles that are outside of God's design is wrong. On the other hand, treating Scripture's boundaries with fear or putting up additional fences can result in a pharisaical and equally wrong approach to ministry among women. Such an approach might even preclude women from assuming any type of decision-making role within the church.

The cost of neglecting the giftedness of women in the local church is far-reaching. Not only will we miss the beauty and joy of a healthy, well-functioning body, but the church will also slowly weaken. The body of Christ is filled with capable women who are eager to serve Christ in the context of the local church, serving under the authority of church leadership. When these women bring their voices and unique gifts to their own communities of believers, the church becomes more and more effective.

Both a young mother with many neighborhood friends and a city councilwoman will have valuable ideas to share about evangelism in their communities. Female real estate attorneys and agents might be a huge asset on a church-building committee. The woman with experience organizing neighborhood co-ops in economically challenged areas and the local bank CEO could both offer their expertise to the congregation in various ways. Many women with teaching gifts will be called to use those gifts in all sorts of biblically appropriate venues. A female church staff member can offer an invaluable role model of biblical training and service, as well as provide an important link between women and church leadership.

Just as women have a responsibility to use their gifts in the local church, so church leaders have a responsibility to welcome their sisters into areas of service within the church where their gifts can be well used. When leadership is proactive in finding ways to incorporate women into various roles, more of the church's rich resources are employed for her work. Our churches are strengthened as women are welcomed to serve profitably and effectively in any area that is not restricted in Scripture.

THEN WHAT?

As Spirit-empowered believers humbly pour their lives into the local church with the goal of building up the body of Christ, an amazing transformation begins to take place. The quirks of some of our brothers and sisters that once drove us crazy begin to fade as our vision for serving and growing the body of Christ takes on definition and focus. We work toward a common goal of worshiping and serving our Father, as his Spirit works among us. Fellow partners in ministry who love God's Word and God's people become treasured friends. We experience the joy of sharing in ministry together, through the highs and lows of our lives. We watch in awe as needs are met that we could never meet by ourselves.

As this transformation occurs (never perfectly, but increasingly), the local church offers the world a living demonstration of the love of Christ—a picture of the gospel. Christ's body is made up of people who are equally unworthy and vastly diverse, learning to forgive and show grace, to love and care for one another—all under the cross of Jesus who loves them, died for them, and offers them resurrection life.

This is what it looks like to be a healthy, well-functioning body of believers. But how do we do this? How do we integrate ministry, and specifically ministry among women, into the life of the church? In general, creating a balanced and beautiful local church community grows out of our shared commitment *to God's Word* and *to one another*. We'll consider first the importance of shared commitment to God's Word.

SHARED COMMITMENT TO GOD'S WORD ENCOURAGES ACCOUNTABILITY

Ministry among women is strengthened through the local church as church leaders encourage sound doctrine, theology, and a focus on teaching and studying the Bible. In chapter 1, Kathleen Nielson highlights the value of Word-centered ministry. This seems basic, and yet our world today—even our Christian world—offers countless pulls in other directions. Being firmly connected to a Bible-based local church offers helpful accountability that protects us from the temptation to drift away from the solid foundation of the gospel as taught in the Word of God.

In his letter to the church in Galatia, Paul warns the early believers concerning the dangers of drifting from the gospel of Christ. He repeatedly condemns the false preachers who lure them away: "As we have said before, so now I say again: If anyone is preaching to you a gospel contrary to the one you received, let him be accursed" (Gal. 1:9). Those are strong words! I'm sure the Galatian believers didn't set out to follow a gospel different from the one Paul taught. But the pressures of life around them gradually pushed them off course and distanced them from Paul's teaching. By the time they received his letter, they were headed in the wrong direction.

A healthy local church is grounded in the vital truths of the gospel of Jesus Christ, with church leaders who ensure that those truths permeate every area of ministry within the church. As the truths of Scripture are proclaimed week after week from the pulpit, God's Word is elevated. Ministries throughout the church naturally begin to reflect that same priority. Hearts that have been gripped by the truths of the gospel become increasingly characterized by the kind of grace and mercy they have experienced. This vital grounding allows church ministries to reflect the priorities of church leadership.

It's easy to become distracted, even in ministries that grow out of a gospel-centered focus. I've had the opportunity to work with a ministry to victims of sex trafficking in the local Chicago area. The physical and emotional needs of these young women can be overwhelming, and in the midst of addressing those it would be easy to lose sight of their deepest needs: the healing love and grace of Jesus Christ as taught in the Scriptures. However, because it exists firmly under the authority of the local church, this ministry reflects the church's priorities; it shares the same DNA. The church's commitment to the gospel helps ensure that the gospel will remain central to the life of this ministry.

SHARED COMMITMENT TO GOD'S WORD ENCOURAGES ONGOING BIBLICAL GROWTH

Marge was a dear friend and partner in ministry. A devoted wife, mother, and grandmother, she divided her boundless energy over the years among Bible study, family, friends, mission trips, politics, outdoor athletics, and art. She was passionate about her art. From etchings on a tiny Fabergé egg to gorgeous dishes for a medieval feast in a Scottish castle, Marge was able to create beauty in multiple categories and on nearly any scale. Marge faithfully invested her artistic gifts in the church through majestic banners, striking floral arrangements, and carefully choreographed Easter services.

Her work was detailed and professional, and it always carried a powerful message.

As a leader in our women's Bible study, Marge brought a fresh and honest approach to our weekly gatherings. She loved the Lord and his Word and was never afraid to ask tough questions about how Scripture relates to everyday life. Her insights deepened our faith. Week after week she would dive deeply into the truths of the Bible. The treasures that she discovered during our times together had a huge impact on the rest of us and on all the rest of her own life and work.

As Marge contributed her gifts and talents, she added a dimension to our congregation that no one else could bring—a dimension we see even more clearly now that Marge is at home with the Lord. Our church is more colorful, more thoughtful, more intricate and beautiful in its design because of her life among us.

As women like Marge (and women learning from women like Marge) come together around God's Word, the fabric of the local church is strengthened. God's Word penetrates hearts and lives. More and more women learn to speak and teach the Word. Truths discovered together begin to spread throughout the church body. Women begin to challenge each other and hold one another accountable, growing together as sisters in Christ. They learn what it means to be godly friends and wives and mothers and employers and employees. They live out Titus 2:3–5. Families become stronger. Deep friendships are developed in the context of ministry. Women grow eager to invest in the life of the church and further the work of the gospel. As women dive deeply into God's Word together, the riches they discover strengthen the local church.

When women hear the truths of God's Word communicated through the voices of other women—joining together around Scripture to study and to pray for one another—strong connections and friendships are built. While growth must take place also in the broader church community, there is a greater freedom to share aspects of life that are unique to women in the context of a ministry specifically for women. When women come together around God's Word, they find not only personal accountability but also deeply shared, ongoing biblical growth.

SHARED COMMITMENT TO ONE ANOTHER ENCOURAGES AUTHENTIC MINISTRY

Out of shared commitment to God's Word grows shared commitment to one another, within the body of Christ. Luke's picture in Acts 2 of the early church offers a striking example of the mutual commitment among believers that characterizes a healthy church, with believers having "all things in common," worshiping and sharing and growing together "with glad and generous hearts" (see Acts 2:44–47).

The church stands in stark contrast to our transient culture, where people are reticent to go all in. In a world where people want to leave all options open and where relationships are dissolved because a friend or spouse fails to "meet my needs," the body of Christ offers a place of stability because of our common and unchanging commitment to Jesus. Among people saved by grace, grace will not stop flowing. Especially as Christian young people are learning the countercultural lessons of marriage as a lifetime commitment, or of perseverance in a challenging job, the example of church members' unceasing care for one another offers a much-needed education in commitment—commitment fueled by God's grace.

As a community of grace-filled believers comes together in a local church, a powerful bonding takes place. Brothers and sisters in Christ filled with the same Spirit unite under shared theology, church governance, and a commitment to one another. In spite of our different personalities, tastes, ages, economic standings, and so forth, we come together by God's grace and through the power of his Spirit to worship our God, to build up our brothers and sisters, and to show the love of Jesus to the world. Of course we never finish learning and repenting and growing in our commitment to this diverse body, but the more we grasp the reality of God's mercy and grace in our own lives, the more our commitment to one another transcends our countless differences.

As this kind of commitment deepens, we grow to appreciate the diversity that characterizes the body of Christ. The church isn't an exclusive club where we come to meet people just like ourselves.

When women's ministry is rooted in the context of the local church, the commitment among believers that permeates the church will flavor the ministry among women. (Of course the effects flow both ways: a women's ministry can help flavor the whole church!) The flavor of shared commitment to one another, with all our differences, is sweet and good. In diverse groups of women, for example, as happened with Nayana, we gain personal glimpses of God's faithfulness in lives that are vastly different from ours. We hear new insights into God's Word. We might learn of struggles common to life among women in contexts foreign to our experiences and perhaps learn also of ways to help and be helped. As we listen to the voices of sisters different from us, we see the greatness of the God we serve.

The relationships formed among a local body of believers are often the deepest and richest of our lives. A seminar in another city or a cross-town Bible study has distinct benefits but many times does not offer the same depth of personal connection as life in the local church, where we have to live out the Word we're studying as we work together on long-term projects, resolve difficulties among ourselves, watch one another's lives and relationships unfold, suffer life and death as one body, and receive the guidance and prayers of our pastors and elders—not just for today, or tomorrow, but for as long as the Lord allows us to be together.

As this deep-seated commitment to one another shapes the hearts and minds of women, ministry is increasingly freed from pretenses. Authenticity grows. Who can keep up a façade for a lifetime? Who would want to anyway? Since we are going to be doing life with each other until the Lord returns or moves us elsewhere, the commitment among a local body of believers allows women the freedom to form strong, authentic relationships built around the truths of God's Word. Ron Bentz describes this reality well: "A healthy church at its core is a group of redeemed Christ followers—recognizing each other's place in God's unfinished church—living in authentic, honest, forgiving, grace-giving community."[4]

The commitment to one another within the local church offers a foundation for authentic ministry among women that grows out of the truths of God's Word.

SHARED COMMITMENT TO ONE ANOTHER ENCOURAGES EVANGELISM

It is this kind of committed community that is best prepared to reach out with the gospel, both teaching the truths of the Word and living them out together as a loving witness. As women in particular pour into the lives of other women, those relationships naturally provide an on-ramp into the life of the church, an avenue through which women can meet Jesus and be welcomed into the local body of Christ.

The early church was characterized by learning from God's Word together, praying together, sharing their means, and doing life with one another. What a unique and exciting community in which to live! As they poured into each other's lives, Luke tells us that "the Lord added to their number day by day those who were being saved" (Acts 2:47b).

A thriving women's ministry offers glimpses of the loving community for which women (and all human beings) yearn. Women who are learning the Word, praying together, enjoying warm fellowship, and caring for the needs of those around them create an inviting community. Visitors to our women's Bible study are regularly drawn into our church community. As they come to know Jesus, women eagerly begin to share the truths of the gospel within their own life contexts. Their enthusiasm for the gospel teaches and inspires all the rest of us. The family of believers multiplies, and the body of Christ is strengthened. My friend Nayana is just one example of many who have blessed our congregation as God has drawn them into our local church through our ministry among women. And women regularly go out from us into all avenues of life better grounded and prepared to share the good news of God's Word with those God puts in their paths.

SHARED COMMITMENT TO ONE ANOTHER
ENCOURAGES HELPFUL AFFIRMATION

Organized ministry among women in the local church offers church leadership (and entire congregations) a context through which they can affirm how much they value and care for their sisters in Christ. When leadership invests in women's ministry, the church communicates to women that their voices are valued and needed. The purpose and significance of their work is affirmed, and the local church is strengthened.

This strengthening takes place as church leadership actively supports ministry by and among women. Communicating a hands-off attitude, by which women are encouraged to "do their own thing," does not help and strengthen women but rather leaves them isolated within the church, perhaps cut off from (and unable to contribute to) the church's vision and momentum. Every ministry, including women's ministry, is strengthened as pastors and elders are engaged, interested, and ready to guide when needed, without being overbearing. This mind-set must be what Peter envisioned in his letter:

So I exhort the elders among you, as a fellow elder and a witness of the sufferings of Christ, as well as a partaker in the glory that is going to be revealed: shepherd the flock of God that is among you, exercising oversight, not under compulsion, but willingly, as God would have you; not for shameful gain, but eagerly; not domineering over those in your charge, but being examples to the flock. (1 Pet. 5:1–3)

There are countless ways that pastors and elders can shepherd and affirm their sisters in Christ who are involved in ministry in the congregation. Many means of affirmation don't require great amounts of time or energy or fanfare. Simply expressing enthusiasm from the pulpit for a women's Bible study or a women's retreat, or sending a brief e-mail before and after an event, or being willing to teach a session or have a consultation when needed, or asking how the elders might be praying, communicates support for what's happening and affirms those involved.

Because of the large number of women who attend our Wednesday morning Bible study, parking is always a challenge. (The Wednesday evening study is not quite so crowded and hard to navigate.) Both studies include women in all stages of life, but the morning one seems to bring an abundance of young mothers who arrive carrying babies, Bibles, diaper bags, purses, and sometimes food to share with their groups. They walk through the doors along with a whole stream of women, some helping the loaded-down ones, some leaning on canes or being pushed along in wheelchairs. It is a lovely but sometimes overwhelming flow of bodies.

Our church pastors and staff recognized the challenges these women face just getting into the building each week. They quietly decided to park off-site on Wednesday mornings, leaving the church parking lot more open for the women who attend Bible study. Such a simple gesture communicates volumes about the church's commitment to women's ministry.

Of course, other more substantive kinds of support speak loudly as well. Many churches are investing funds in various kinds of training for women Bible teachers, whether holding training classes that are available to women and men, or sending women teachers/leaders to workshops or conferences, or paying for online courses, or supporting staff women in seminary study. The number of paid female staff in strong evangelical churches is slowly growing. In complementarian circles, when we're clear about the few things God has not called women to do, God's people can pursue wholeheartedly the support and encouragement of the countless things women can do.

But what if there is no women's ministry in our local church? Or if this strong connection between church leadership and women's ministry is not a reality? How does God's Word inform our approach to ministry in that setting? The writer of Hebrews addresses the relationship between church leaders and those under their care:

> Obey your leaders and submit to them, for they are keeping watch over your souls, as those who will have to give an account. Let them do this with joy and not with groaning, for that would be of no advantage to you. (Heb. 13:17)

Our pastors and elders shoulder an enormous responsibility before the Lord. As members under their care, we are called to pray for them and to submit to their leadership in a way that brings them joy and not "groaning."

This doesn't mean we women shouldn't approach our pastors and/or elders with our concerns or with our visions related to ministry among women within the church. That is our responsibility! But the words of Hebrews do need to define our attitude. Our approach to women's ministry must be characterized by humility and respect for the role that the Lord has given to those in authority over us.

We can begin by carefully considering the vision that the church leadership has established for our own local body of believers. We can ask questions like, "How might our vision for women support and further the goals of our local church?" We can initiate conversations with leadership, together seeking how women's ministries might best fit into our own church context. We can respectfully seek to communicate with our leaders ways that ministry among women could serve as an extension of their care for God's people.

Above all, we must be prayerful, waiting upon the Lord to make the way clear. Flexibility and patience will surely be required as we receive answers and timelines that might not be in line with our initial vision. We can trust the Lord to accomplish his purposes through our efforts by doing a work that is different and ultimately even more effective than our original plans. The church belongs to the Lord, and he will be faithful.

By God's grace, vibrant women's ministry in a local congregation committed to God's Word and to each other will strengthen not just the women within that church community but the whole church body as well and ultimately the whole church.

A WORTHWHILE INVESTMENT

So is it really worth the significant effort to ground women's ministry clearly and securely within the context of the local church? Absolutely. Will it bring challenges that we might rather avoid? Most certainly. Will it mean working alongside women who are strikingly different from us? Quite likely. Will it mean submitting our ideas and our dreams to the authority of our church leadership? Yes. Will it be uncomfortable? Sometimes.

But it will also mean investing our God-given gifts as women in the context in which our Father intended them to be used. It means pouring out our lives for our brothers and sisters who love Jesus. It means growing to love them and appreciate them for who they are in Christ and who they are becoming, as they grow in the Word.

Ministering as women in the local church means learning together to reach out with the good news of the gospel. It means actively loving the growing body of Christ—the very community that Christ loves—the bride for which he gave his life.

At the end of time, as we celebrate the great wedding feast of the Lamb, we will discover that our investment in the bride of Christ was worth every painful interaction, every sleepless night, and every unnoticed act of service. And together with all our brothers and sisters, we will spend eternity in praise and worship of the one who gave his life for us.

— 5 —

The World around Us

Practicing Evangelism

Gloria Furman

My aim in this chapter is to demonstrate why women's ministry that is grounded in Bible study effectively carries out the Great Commission. The first explanation that comes to mind is that I personally owe my eternal gratitude to God for such a ministry.

I WANT TO REACH THE LOST. WHITHER BIBLE STUDY?

Jamie cast the net wide that afternoon on a college campus. Herself a university student, she approached a group of us freshman girls and asked if we were Christians. I identified myself as such. It was my understanding that because I had been raised in a Christian country, did not worship any foreign gods, had attended church as a child with my parents, and believed God was real, that made me a Christian.

Jamie invited my friends and me to a fun event hosted by the college ministry of a local church. There was music, food, and lots of coffee. That evening I met some older collegians who invited me to join a freshman girls Bible study. In the swirling sea of unfamiliar faces at university, I was so happy to have been found by such wonderful and genuine people! In the weeks that followed I faithfully attended Bible study and completed the work assigned in the Gospel of John. It was there, through my careful study of the Bible in the context of community, that I discovered *I was actually lost.* My Bible study leader had the care and concern to challenge my assumption that I was a Christian, and she helped me understand that my upbringing and culture had nothing to do with being born again in Jesus Christ. Passages from our Bible study in John, such as Jesus's interaction with Nicodemus and the woman at the well, all of a sudden made sense to me. My friend shared with me the good news of Christ's atoning sacrifice on the cross on my behalf, and by God's grace I believed it.

Even though my testimony is not rare by any means, I understand that many women have reservations about inviting nonbelievers to study the Bible with them. Some of the misconceptions I have heard doubting the effectiveness of evangelistic Bible study are as follows:

- The best (or only) material for nonbelievers to engage is apologetics specific to their religious or cultural background.

- Confusing or controversial doctrine must be watered down (or banned) if you study the Bible with a nonbeliever, in order to put Christianity's best face forward.

- Mature believers cannot grow spiritually in Bible studies in which nonbelievers participate.

- Inductive Bible study is too difficult for nonbelievers to understand, so addressing their felt needs through topical dialogues or passive learning methods is the best place to start.

- The good news is more difficult to discern in certain books (or genres) of the Bible, so nonbelievers may be invited to Bible studies only if one of the Gospels is being studied.

- What makes a Bible study evangelistic is that the teacher shares the gospel at the end of the time together.

- Nonbelievers have many sin issues (addictions, immorality, unbelief, etc.) that need to be dealt with first before they can appropriately receive God's Word through Bible study.

- The Bible is of no real interest to nonbelievers, so why are we even having this conversation?

Perhaps the misconception that takes the cake of absurdity is this one: "Women are feelers and not thinkers, so Bible study is pointless, especially with nonbelieving women, who do not have the mind of Christ."

With all these misconceptions about Bible study and evangelism (and women!) swirling around, is it appropriate for us to be confident that Bible study is a blessing to the nonbelieving women in our lives? If we endeavor to strike into these so-called ambiguous waters, how can we be assured that a Bible study is trustworthy for evangelism and will carry us to the shore? Isn't Bible study primarily for building up the maturity of those who are already believers? Is there a best place to start in Bible study when hoping to engage nonbelievers? How is Bible study relevant to the desperate situations that our nonbelieving friends are in? Doesn't a blasé academic exercise such as Bible study put a damper on evangelistic enthusiasm? Bible study seems like a rather impotent tool in the ministry tool belt when we think of women who are hurting. Can we trust that Bible study is a clear and understandable means for sharing the gospel with these women? Is the same true for verse-by-verse, inductive Bible studies? What if we're studying 2 Kings 2:24 that day? Are nonbelievers even interested in Bible study, making this conversation a moot point?

Our misconceptions need clarity, and our questions require answers. I believe it is an overwhelming encouragement to consider that even in light of various pragmatic solutions, we need look no further than God's Word for the clarity and answers we seek.

The main question I will address in this chapter is: *What does Bible study have to do with our mission to reach women for Christ?* The answer I will defend is a comprehensive "Everything!" Lest readers fear they may never reach the end of this chapter, I have limited my argument to a few specific points. For the purposes of this book I have also limited my discussion to the context of Bible study among women, although certainly these effects of Bible study are at work in various ways in various contexts.

1. Bible study fuels our evangelistic zeal.
2. Bible study equips healthy ambassadors.
3. Bible study marks the spot for all of us: You Are Here!
4. Bible study shows us God.
5. Bible study turns guests into hosts.

BIBLE STUDY FUELS OUR EVANGELISTIC ZEAL

How can we gain a passion for winning souls? Before we answer this question positively, I think it is useful to understand what will *not* enflame our hearts for evangelism. We do not feel inclined to invite others to the banqueting feast if we are standing off to the side sipping a cup of lukewarm pond water. When we are not being nourished by God's life-giving Word, we find that we have little enthusiasm to share his Word with others.

But what happens when we feel like the psalmist? "My soul is consumed with longing for your rules [just decrees] at all times" (Ps. 119:20). What happens when we are hungry for the bread that

Jesus claims will satisfy forever (John 6:51–58)? We crave the bread of life that satisfies forever. We learn about him in his Word. "I open my mouth and pant, because I long for your commandments" (Ps. 119:131). Spreading worship of the risen Christ through evangelism is a reflex of having tasted and seen his goodness in God's Word. When the Holy Spirit enlivens our hearts to the sweet satisfaction of all that Jesus is for us and in us, then we can't help but speak of him!

Contrary to any misconceptions, women who are engaged in Bible study are actually *being equipped* for the good work of evangelism and mission, not distracted from it. God breathed his Word in order to make us complete for these things and not lacking the teaching, reproof, correction, and training we need to obey the Great Commission (Matt. 28:18–20; 2 Tim. 3:16–17).

In addition to all the equipping we need for reaching the lost, the Bible itself fuels our zeal to see God's name treasured among the nations. I am privileged to see this happen among women all the time in my local church, which in God's providence is a meeting place of people from many nations. The women's evangelism naturally flows through their Bible studies with one another as they instinctively invite nonbelieving women in their lives to share the treasure they've found. This happens in informal settings in living rooms with toddlers ambling about their feet as they talk about Scripture with their neighbors and in organized studies that meet for a defined time period to study a specific book. These women are like the Samaritan woman at the well who testified, "Come, see" (John 4:29).

I have heard women lament that they wish they shared their faith with others more. We may feel disappointed in our lack of passion for winning souls. Perhaps we grow discouraged in sharing the gospel because of the enemy's accusations against our integrity. Indeed, many of us have lost our own wonder at the fact that we are known by God. Our heavenly Father knows and understands the frailty of our hearts, and Jesus is sympathetic to our weaknesses, having been clothed in human flesh forever. Some good news about sharing the good news with others is that God is faithful to set our hearts ablaze with affections for him that are greater than anything we might desire on this earth. Scottish pastor Thomas Chalmers referred to this as "the expulsive power of a new affection."[1] In other words, when your delight is in the Lord, he becomes the desire of your heart. Our timid hearts have no reason to fear that our gracious God might hold himself aloof from those who seek his face day and night.

This is true for us who have been adopted into his forever family and for those lost sheep whom Jesus is seeking. Surely he is both willing and able to satisfy the longings of those who want to taste and see his goodness. When we are engaged in Bible study, we find ourselves steeped in the joy of having found "that one thing" that cannot be taken away from us.

> Trust in the Lord, and do good;
> > dwell in the land and befriend faithfulness.
> Delight yourself in the Lord,
> > and he will give you the desires of your heart. (Ps. 37:3–4)

God created us and our neighbors to be food-dependent creatures so that we would have an idea of what Jesus meant when he said, "I am the living bread that came down from heaven. If anyone eats of this bread, he will live forever. And the bread that I will give for the life of the world is my flesh" (John 6:51). The simplicity and priority of engaging our unbelieving friends, neighbors, and both near and far unreached people groups with the Word of God are clear. Jesus aims to satisfy us with himself forever, and it is through his living and active Word that he offers the revelation of himself that makes us "wise for salvation through faith in Christ Jesus" (2 Tim. 3:15).

When the idea of opening up God's Word with my nonbelieving friends is intimidating to me, for whatever reason, I have been personally encouraged by the idea that I am simply one hungry woman telling other hungry women where to find the bread of life. More than one person is served in more ways than one. Yes, my nonbelieving friends have an opportunity to hear the living God speak through his Word when I open the Bible with them, but I am also dually blessed. Rather than remaining consumed with my own wants, needs, and issues in my study of the Bible, talking about God's Word with other women serves to reorient my focus outward in worship to God and in service to others. I also get to live out the priority of feeding myself before I attempt to feed others—just as flight attendants remind passengers to secure their own oxygen mask first.

"It's like a whirlwind; it just sucks them in!" A missionary spoke about the excitement of seeing what happens when she directs her neighbors to read God's Word for themselves. On one particular occasion she advised her friend to begin reading in the Gospel of Luke, but the next time they met her friend began to fire away her questions based on what she had read in the book of Acts. "I'm sorry I've miscommunicated," the missionary apologized. "I should have bookmarked Luke for you. Your questions are from Acts, a different book." Her friend replied, "Yes, I read Luke, but I couldn't stop reading." God's living and active Word spoke to this woman, and she felt compelled to read more and more—and the missionary felt encouraged to share the Word more and more boldly. I do not know whether her friend has become a Christian, but her story reminds us that the Bible is not a static collection of stories about God. God's Word *is* God speaking. We dare not treat Bible study or Scripture reading as a mere tool in our evangelism toolbox. God's Word is not simply *at the heart of* what we want to say to our nonbelieving friends and neighbors; it is what they must know and what we can be thrilled to offer.

Her story also demonstrates the absurdity of the supposition that women are categorically uninterested in and unequipped for the rigors of Bible study.

Bible study keeps our zeal grounded in the un-adjustable truth contained in the gospel. Even in the plurality of contexts of living missionally all over the world, the message we proclaim must remain the same. Perhaps the greatest (and most destructive) temptations regarding mission lie in assuming or even distorting the gospel message. We read in Romans 1:1–6 that the message is God's gospel: *God decides the good news that we need*. This gospel is concerning the person and work of his Son, Jesus: *God defines the content of the message*. The goal of God's gospel is to bring about obedience of faith for the sake of his name among all nations: *God determines the outcome of his good news being believed*. By God's grace, our commitment to proclaim the one and only life-giving gospel must never waver. Also by God's grace, our willingness to be used by God for his mission should be pliable and sensitive to his Spirit. Where else can we understand these things but in the study of his eternal Word?

In God's Word we understand that Christ ascended back into heaven while he was still in the flesh, and his incarnation endures forever. Compelled by the love of this Christ, local churches walk in the power of his Spirit in all our evangelistic efforts. Resisting the urge to gather only with women who look like us, live in homes like ours, consume products or wear brands like we do, we freely share the gospel with anyone without exception, prejudice, or envy. In God's Word we read about how the eternal Son was pleased to clothe himself in our human flesh, and we see that it is fitting for us as God's chosen ones to put on compassionate hearts toward *all* men and women (Col. 3:12). Our zeal for evangelism is fueled by our heart's apprehension of these truths as the Holy Spirit stokes the fires of our affections for Christ and his Word.

HEALTHY AMBASSADORS NEED BIBLE STUDY

Jesus said, "Peace be with you. As the Father has sent me, even so I am sending you" (John 20:21). He has commissioned us as his sent ones, ambassadors who bear the announcement that God has granted amnesty to all who cling to him by faith. The evangelistic overflow from our Bible studies among women will look different across the globe. Spirit-empowered "Word work" is happening among disciples of Jesus everywhere—among villagers in Quezon City, midwives in Lagos, hotel managers in São Paolo, and grandmothers in Chapel Hill. We have every reason to rejoice in the diversity of our ministries among women all over the world because the indwelling Holy Spirit distributes gifts to each of us according to his will (Heb. 2:4). You will notice a sampling of testimonies about this aspect of ministry among women in the chapter on giftedness (see chapter 9).

Since Christ's commission to us assumes that his body will live on mission together, it must be his Spirit who empowers us in our efforts to work in tandem as we flex the muscles of Christian discipleship. The triunity of the God who has given us eternal life, commissioned us, and equipped us for ministry, is one massive reason for us to lay aside our skepticism of other women based on surface-level differences. We are gathered together, built up, and equipped so that we can be scattered to the corners of the earth, bearing his message of good news. I think of the somewhat involuntary reflex of the international churches that are filled with "elect exiles" (1 Pet. 1:1), expatriate believers who find themselves transplanted in new cities all over the world every few years because of the nature of their work. They are brought into a new place and (Lord willing) plugged into a local church where they are discipled and disciple others—particularly through Bible study, so key to spiritual formation in the context of community. Then, seemingly just as they get started in one city, they are launched out to another, taking the gospel with them. It's the rhythm university students know well, as they settle in only to be sent out.

Women have unique contributions to make in this kind of cross-cultural work simply because they are women. How women are viewed in different regions of the world varies widely. What incredible opportunities women have to speak the truth in love to other women who have never heard that God made women in his image and that he regards them as precious and valuable to him! I'm thinking particularly of the many cultural contexts in which it is appropriate for *only* women to engage in friendships with other women. Especially when placed in such contexts we do not mourn the loss of opportunity to reach out to men, but we are instead focused on the task the Lord has given us (a mighty task) to reach out to women, ready to spread the seed of the Word that has been planted in us.

The organic going and sending of Christ's people everywhere and in every life season are facilitated by the indwelling Spirit, who guides and directs us. I personally treasure the many occasions on which other women visited me in my home to bring me meals when my babies were born. In addition to helping provide physically for my growing family, these women would pray with me, and we would share fellowship together perhaps over what I missed in that week's Bible study or sermon at church. As a result I am now more prepared to take the Word to others, wherever I am planted. Word-filled women minister to one another in all our contexts because we are walking by the Spirit, who breathed out that Word in the first place. We take with us the message we have been given, which is God's Word—cherished, believed, obeyed, and meditated on day and night. The message of hope for the nations, the strength for ministry, and the comfort in our troubles along the way belong to *all* of us in the body of Christ. What a glorious privilege we have to pass on these treasures as Spirit-filled women, uniquely designed and gifted by God to the praise of his glory.

BIBLE STUDY MARKS THE SPOT FOR US: YOU ARE HERE!

Is there any other avenue in ministry where we more often get to see souls revived and hearts strengthened? It is a remarkable thing to be in a Bible study as a firsthand witness when someone realizes that the story of her life—*her* life—is actually a part of The Greatest Story. We imagine that our life contains plot twists and surprises, and we wonder to ourselves, "Was this moment the climax? Or was that it?" It is a fair question to ask, and one that the Bible makes clear. When we take care to incorporate biblical theology into our study of the Bible, the centrality of the gospel emerges on every page. What a shock it is to us when we see in the Scriptures that the climax of our lives has already happened—at the cross and at that empty tomb! And what an incredible prospect it is when we realize the eternal implications of our destiny in Christ Jesus. This is the big story that makes sense of all our little ones.

From the sixty-six books of the Bible emerges a single narrative about God's mission to establish a kingdom for his Son where he will reign forever with the bride whom he has purchased and purified for himself. When we help others follow the plotline of the Bible, with Jesus Christ shining forth as the main character from beginning to end, then the gospel is beautifully clarified through all the various genres the Lord has given us in his understandable Word. All the promises of God, themes, and typology in Scripture throw spotlights onto the stage of history to reveal the crucified, risen, and ascended Lord of glory as the center of all things.

Consider the temple of God as just one example, one strand of the storyline that stretches through the Bible and makes us long for the place of God's presence. God created the garden of Eden for Adam and Eve to dwell in, and he walked with them there. However, because of their sin God expelled Adam and Eve from his holy presence and stationed an angel with a flaming sword to guard the entrance to the garden. Later in the Bible we read about the tabernacle, a temporary locale prescribed by God to be his dwelling place among his people. Then once Israel occupied the Promised Land, the Lord came in a cloud of glory to dwell in the Most Holy Place in the temple in Jerusalem (1 Kings 8:10–11). His presence with them was made possible by his provision of the sacrificial system: priests daily offered sacrifices on behalf of a sinful people. The temple was destroyed when their kingdom fell, and through their captivities and exiles God's people lamented (and sometimes forgot) that the Lord no longer dwelled among them in his holy temple.

But the story wasn't over. The returned exiles rebuilt the temple and waited. And God came—but this time not in a cloud. Jesus Christ came, stood in the temple, and made a statement that knocked the people off their rockers: "Destroy this temple, and in three days I will raise it up" (John 2:19). Those who heard him assumed he was making an audacious claim about the building, but he was referring to his body (John 2:21). Jesus is God in the flesh; he tabernacled among us—lived, died on the cross as the perfect sacrifice, and rose again. Through faith in Jesus the people of God are gathered together into the "body of Christ," which is the temple of the Holy Spirit (1 Cor. 3:16–17; Eph. 2:19–22). Another idea that knocked people off their rockers (and still does today in certain parts of our world) is that women are included in this holy gathering of God's people. Through the indwelling Holy Spirit, Jesus dwells in us and among us so that he can claim, "Behold, I am with you always, to the end of the age" (Matt. 28:20). The Bible points us to look forward to the end of the age when there will be a garden city not made with human hands, and in that place will be the throne of God and of the Lamb, and his servants will worship him (Rev. 22:1–5). There will be no temple there, for "its temple is the Lord God the Almighty and the Lamb," Rev. 21:22). We—both men and women—will see God's face because he will dwell among us forever and ever. From Genesis to Revelation, from creation to re-creation, the story holds together.

The author of history graciously intervened in our lives while we were yet sinners and died for us on the cross (Rom. 5:8). That's the climax of the story. The crucifixion of the Son of God—the turning point of the history of humanity—is our turning point too. The rescue plan that was devised in the utterly holy counsel of the triune Godhead was set in motion before any of us were ever born. Now our gracious God commands all people everywhere to repent, because he has fixed a day on which he will judge the world in righteousness by a man whom he has appointed; and of this he has given assurance to all by raising him from the dead (Acts 17:30–31). Careful study of Scripture allows our nonbelieving friends to see the big picture and understand where they are in light of God's story of redemption.

Think of the ongoing barrage of messages the world sends to women about who they are, what they are to do, and how they might be fulfilled. And think of the vast trove of wisdom in God's Word that awaits women who are starved to know God's eternal and good purposes for them, to give them along with all God's people hope, future, and dignity. And just think of how this new eternity-aware worldview ejects us from the tiny little worlds we have holed ourselves up in. This same eye-opening through the Word will also happen for our sisters who have yet to hear and respond to the gospel.

How would it change the way our nonbelieving friends viewed the Bible if they understood that they were part of *the* story? Can you imagine their delight when they realize the narrative that God has for women is worlds different from that of this world, which is passing away? What might they realize about the relevance of Scripture to their daily (and eternal) lives? How would this new perspective change the way they view their sexuality, or their motherhood, or their singleness, or their aging process? Where could the Spirit of God send them with this message of reconciliation to God—to the flat next door, the high-rise on the other side of the world, the office down the hall, their own homes?

We must let our friends see the big picture of biblical theology. Clarity bursts forth with shining brilliance out of foggy confusion when we teach that the so-called random stories in the Bible actually serve to collectively point us to the greatest (and only) story. I have a friend from an Eastern country who said that it is a custom in her culture to send condolences to a new mother who gives birth to a daughter. This anecdote may sound dramatic to Western ears, but consider the implications of the tongue-in-cheek remark to new fathers of daughters: "Guess you'd better buy a shotgun for future would-be suitors." In every part of the world, women desperately need to hear how a biblical worldview informs the way they view themselves. What better place to learn about this radically different mind-set, and to ask questions in a safe environment, than in a Bible study among other women?

Biblical theology reveals The Greatest Story in all of its high-definition grandeur. At once you want to lean back and take it all in while you are simultaneously obsessed with each of the tiny pixels you can spot. Aspects of our personhood woven into the very fabric of who we are, such as the fact that God created us as his gendered image bearers, come into focus. By God's grace we can help our nonbelieving friends and family spot themselves in God's story through the study of his Word. When they begin to see with the eyes of their hearts, may the God who said, "Let light shine out of darkness," shine in their hearts to give the light of the knowledge of his glory in the face of Jesus Christ (2 Cor. 4:6).

BIBLE STUDY SHOWS US GOD

God's awe-full holiness is beautiful to those who have hidden themselves in Jesus Christ, the one mediator between God and man (1 Tim. 2:5). But to those who are outside of Christ, spiritually dead while they yet live, the holiness of God is inconceivable horror. We need to recognize and utilize the evangelistic nature of Bible study because our lost friends need to see God and live. But so long as they remain outside of Christ, they cannot see God and live. We all have the same problem: our sin separates us from our holy creator, God, who has declared, "Man shall not see me and live" (Ex. 33:20). The sinking sensation we get in the pit of our stomach from having our sin found out by another sinful human being is but a tiny fraction of the terror that human beings feel when they realize they have beheld the glory of the living God.[2] Our sin separates us from God and brings God's righteous judgment and eternal punishment.

Confessing that sin in a place where they are confident (or perhaps at least hopeful) that they will be met by empathetic listening ears is a high value for many women. How many times I have been in Bible studies with other women who have taken those occasions as opportunities to confess sin in the presence of believers who can turn them to the Savior. These conversations have been facilitated by the Word of God, which shines its light into the dark places of our hearts. The Spirit of God uses the Word as his instrument of conviction, edification, pruning, instruction, and rebuke, which ultimately leads to abundant life and fruit bearing. Word-filled women have a particular gift for helping along other women who are seeing God in his Word and seeing themselves in light of that Word, wrestling through sin issues, and battling temptation.

Our neighbors, coworkers, relatives, and other dear ones will one day face the Holy One of Israel, and we know where they can find the unhindered access into the throne room of heaven that they will need on that day. We have the privilege of heralding God's good news concerning his Son. We get to respond to his call to pour out our lives in order to make this announcement:

Go on up to a high mountain,
    O Zion, herald of good news;
lift up your voice with strength,
    O Jerusalem, herald of good news;
lift it up, fear not;
    say to the cities of Judah,
"Behold your God!" (Isa. 40:9)

How is it possible that sinful men and women could behold God and live? Jesus said in his Sermon on the Mount, "Blessed are the pure in heart, for they shall see God" (Matt. 5:8). But none of us is righteous, *not even one* (Ps. 14:10; Rom. 3:10–12). Even the most unassuming and gentle women, the most religiously pious women, and the well-to-do women who look as though they have need of nothing *all* need this one thing if they are to see God and live: grace. Where does this grace come from? It comes from the gospel—the gospel that is heralded, explained, defended, and rejoiced over in our study of the Bible. According to his Word, God himself has made a way for us and for all his called-out people to see his face and live, and the exclusive means for us to experience this unspeakable joy is through Jesus Christ and his atoning work on the cross alone.

For God, who said, "Let light shine out of darkness," has shone in our hearts to give the light of the knowledge of the glory of God in the face of Jesus Christ. (2 Cor. 4:6)

The very sight of Christ's glory in the cross transforms us (2 Cor. 3:18), and this is the work of God's Holy Spirit. In our Bible studies we have opportunity after opportunity to see how the triune God has torn asunder every barricade, every obstacle, and every threat to our happiness in him. The Old Testament anticipates this liberation. In the Gospels, Jesus announces that he is the Messiah who has come to set the captives free. In Acts and the Epistles we see how this freedom is lived out in the power of the indwelling Spirit. John's apocalyptic vision in Revelation shows us that because of what Jesus has done for us on the cross, we can look forward to the day that Christ appears and ushers in an eternity with God where the promise is fulfilled: "They will see his face" (Rev. 22:4).

We can and we must invite others to see what we see in God's Word in order to make our joy complete (1 John 1:1–4). In our Bible studies we gather to be fed, but let's also remember that being fed is a means to feed others too.

> Let us know; let us press on to know the LORD;
>> his going out is sure as the dawn;
> he will come to us as the showers,
>> as the spring rains that water the earth. (Hos. 6:3)

When that dawn breaks and forever day begins, we will stand next to generations of men, women, and children from next door to across the globe singing to the praise of his glorious grace:

> Salvation belongs to our God who sits on the throne, and to the Lamb! (Rev. 7:10)

I love to think of the women whom God has sovereignly brought into my sphere of influence and pray for each of them, asking God for opportunities to share his life-giving words with them. What about the women *you* know? Look across your driveway, living room, or cubicle, and wonder *who* might be your hope or joy or crown of boasting before our Lord Jesus at his coming (1 Thess. 2:19)? By God's grace, it may be the woman who just came to your mind.

BIBLE STUDY TURNS GUESTS INTO HOSTS

There is no need to feel skittish or insecure about inviting nonbelievers into our fellowship and study of the Bible. We need to shift away from our false consumer guilt when it comes to the banqueting feast of God's Word and fellowship with his body. The reason for this is that the eager anticipation we have when we come together for fellowship around God's Word says true things about God. It says that he is our Good Shepherd, in whose care we have no need for want. It says that the pastures he leads us to are full of rich fare to restore our soul. It says that we have a need for his leadership in paths of righteousness and his comfort in the valley of the shadow of death. It says that his presence dissuades our fears and his fatherly discipline corrects us. It says that he is the one who can satisfy us and make certain that we are secure in his love forever. There is no place for our false consumer guilt because we cannot add to God and his Word; we can only receive.

Understanding the satisfaction we humbly receive from the person of Christ and his Word, which is our food, it only makes sense that we should invite anyone and everyone to come and have their cups filled to overflowing also. Not one of us can live by bread alone, but we all have need to taste and see that Jesus, the bread of life (John 6:48), is good. "For the bread of God is he who comes down from heaven and gives life to the world" (John 6:33). What better place for someone who is curious or even skeptical to pull up a chair to the feast than in the company of revelers who know how good the fare is? When people find something good, they tell others about it.

CONCLUDING THOUGHTS

Bible study should not be thought of as an optional, peripheral arm for reaching women with the gospel. Bible study is as core to soul winning as the digestive system is to fueling the body. The deeper we dig into the meaning of God's Word, the more closely we can follow after God and draw near to the one who revealed himself to us as "the way." Through careful Bible study we may arrive at knowledge of the truth that points us to the one who revealed himself to us as "the truth." It follows that in our diligent study of the Bible we receive sustenance from the Word, who revealed himself to us as "the life" (John 14:6).

In the university women's Bible study where I became a Christian, I was introduced to *the life*, shown his *way*, and taught his *truth*. As I dove into the feast laid before me in God's Word, he changed me from an agnostic guest to an enthusiastic hostess, inviting more and more women to come taste and see God's goodness.

We Christians affirm that the Bible is to be received as the authoritative Word of God, and we deny that the Scriptures receive their authority from the church, tradition, or any other human source.[3] Since the Bible is not just a collection of words about God, but God's self-revealing Word, we cannot possibly overvalue its worth in our personal endeavor to know God and to introduce him to those who don't know him. Since faith comes from hearing, and hearing through the word of Christ (Rom. 10:17), we may have outlandish confidence in urging others to join us in expecting and praying for many to come to faith in Christ as we study his Word together.

Millions and millions of people in the world have not yet or cannot practically (or legally) avail themselves of the benefits given to us by the Reformers, some of whom gave their lives so that we could have access to God's Word. While we have life and breath, it is our happy duty to give ourselves to Great Commission discipleship, which includes helping the Scriptures become accessible and understandable to everyone. What might the Spirit do through Word-filled women whose rock-steady assurance is in the God who gave us his Word? Our ministry of reconciliation (2 Cor. 5:18) would subsume every aspect of our ministry among women.

Grounded in the Word of God and out of the overflow of the joy we have from being reconciled to God in Christ, we plead with fellow sinners to repent and believe the gospel: "Friend, what will you do with your sin? 'But who can endure the day of his coming, and who can stand when he appears?' (Mal. 3:2). Where will you find true and lasting hope and peace? I want you to come to the cross with me. How we all so desperately need him! 'For Christ is the end of the law for righteousness to everyone who believes' (Rom. 10:4). 'The Spirit and the Bride say, "Come." And let the one who hears say, "Come." And let the one who is thirsty come; let the one who desires take the water of life without price' (Rev. 22:17). Be reconciled to God through Christ. There is no other way to the Father. Won't you come with me to Jesus?"

We were made to live by God's Word and to live forever, at that! As far as we are able, we must take God's Word as seriously as it takes itself when we are studying it with one another and with our nonbelieving friends. We should do so with expectancy, because when the Spirit of God illumines Scripture and gives people ears to hear, then the waters of eternal life will spring forth in the wilderness. Jesus said, "If anyone thirsts, let him come to me and drink. Whoever believes in me, as the Scripture has said, 'Out of his heart will flow rivers of living water'" (John 7:37–38). Thirsty for Jesus, we drink in his life-sustaining Word. When our thirst is quenched, we can't help but turn to those around us and invite them to come and see the man (John 4:29). When that happens, may our various ministries among women be equipped to dive right in.

— 6 —

The Ends of the Earth

Thinking Global

Keri Folmar

What kind of ministry helps HIV-positive mothers who are living in poverty? How can evangelism be encouraged in a country where proselytization is illegal and conversion is punishable by death? How does a church with members from many different countries cultivate unity among women from contrasting cultures?

The issues that arise in churches around the world are as varied as the cultures in which they arise. And the ways women minister among and to one another are as diverse as the different cultures where they minister. The day-to-day issues and methods will indeed differ from one country to the next, but the most fruitful ministries among women across the globe have three things in common: *saturation in the Word of God, clarity about the gospel, and connection with the local church.*

Fruitful ministry happens when women saturate themselves in the Word of God, knowing that the Bible speaks in every culture and stage of life. It happens when women are caught up in the glory of the gospel, and that clear message motivates and informs their lives and ministry. It happens when women are fully engaged in the life of a Bible-believing, gospel-preaching church, bringing their needs and using their gifts for the good of the local body of Christ. In this chapter we'll explore these components of healthy women's ministry, and we'll listen to the international voices of those who are joyfully and fruitfully serving the Lord.

SATURATION IN THE WORD OF GOD

The Bible was written out of an ancient Middle Eastern culture, but far from being tied to a particular people during a particular period of history, the words speak into every culture at every period of time. This is because, while there are many human authors of Scripture, there is one divine author. "Men spoke from God as they were carried along by the Holy Spirit" (2 Pet. 1:21). God has revealed himself in his Word and in it given us all we need to live our lives for him. "All Scripture is breathed out by God and profitable for teaching, for reproof, for correction, and for training in righteousness, that the man [or woman] of God may be complete, equipped for every good work" (2 Tim. 3:16–17). This living and active Word speaks to the variety of issues faced by women in churches in the North, South, East, and West. It is important for each of us in our own little parts of the world—and it is exciting as well—to see God's Word at work in and through women around the world. Listen to what Yuri Ayliffe from Japan has to say about God's Word at work in her church:

> I come from a totally non-Christian background in Japan. I
> didn't grow up in the environment where Christian worldview

was the norm. So when I came to faith at the age of twenty-three, there was so much I didn't understand about the Bible and how it fits together, how it helps me to understand God, man, and God's will for me. The Lord graciously led me to a church where the Word of God was faithfully taught on every possible occasion.

I attended ladies' Bible study where we go through books of the Bible season after season in an inductive Bible study style. This helped me to understand what the Word means, and it also helped me to see how to do this at home. I wrestled with many portions of the Bible I didn't understand, yet it's like every time that pieces of the puzzle fit together, one by one, it gives me amazement of how truly beautiful the Word of God is. How perfect and flawless.

Coming together with other sisters weekly also helped me be accountable for what I am learning and saying. It showed me how the church plays an important role in my Christian walk. We challenge one another as we reflect on God's Word together in earnest prayer and with seeking hearts. I saw our lives constantly changing, growing in his grace. Our foundation was the Word of God, and that alone by the power of his Spirit. We learned together how we need the gospel on a daily basis as we discover truth together. I saw humility in mature ladies and realized that it is an ongoing, joyful endeavor to walk with God. I saw many women using their gifts in various capacities, some in public, some at home, and some in church. Our love for one another grew along with our love for the Savior. The Word of God is indeed bread of heaven to our souls. We need fresh supply every day.

Some say that Asian cultures are geared toward storytelling and don't connect with straightforward biblical teaching, but Yuri has thrived under Bible-saturated ministry, empowered by the Holy Spirit. And how wonderful that Scripture is full of narratives, stories through which God reveals himself! Regardless of where women grow and minister, we should keep the Word as our firm foundation. Women hear ungodly messages from the world around them all week long. No matter which country we live in, most of us are often surrounded by alluring advertisements, unedifying musical lyrics, and unwholesome speech. We need to have our weeks interrupted by God's Word. We need to hear right preaching of the Word, and we need to hear the teaching and speaking of the Word. Good women's ministries—wherever they are—aim to bring a message that breaks through the chaotic noise pollution of the day. As 2 Timothy 3:16–17 tells us, women are equipped by the Word of God; therefore, our Bible studies, discipling, hospitality, and outreach must be saturated with it.

Bible Study

To say that women's Bible studies should be saturated with the Word of God sounds painfully obvious. But, sadly, Bible studies can be sidetracked by other things—even good things. They can become social clubs where fellowship is the primary goal, and the focus is on the food served rather than the bread of life. They can become counseling sessions where troubled women come to get their felt needs met. Or they can be places where women are entertained by videos of enthusiastic, well-intentioned teachers who, in an effort to be relevant, miss the point of the text being studied. Fellowship, counseling, and meeting felt needs are some of the fruit of a good Bible study as women deepen in their relationships with one another and conform their lives to the Word. And Bible study leaders and teachers should be enthusiastic and joyful about the Word in a way that overflows into the lives of others. However, these things should never supplant focused and deep study of the Bible, because it is the Scriptures that have the power to change lives (Ps. 119:129).

Martha Makuku at Kibera Reformed Presbyterian Church in

Kenya calls the Word of God "vital." KRPC holds a women's Bible study every Wednesday for women of all ages, most of them unmarried, heads of their households, although some are second or third wives. These women live in severe poverty, often going without food and basic life essentials. About half are HIV-positive. Martha says,

> The culture in my context is very complicated because the community consists of women from different tribes, and each tribe has its own culture. What could be working against one tribe could be a strength in another culture. One culture could be matriarchal and another patriarchal. Harmony is found only in Scripture, and our goal in the Bible study is to foster a biblical culture that gives us a new identity in Christ while rejecting sin.

This focus on the Scriptures has cultivated a strong sense of community among the women in the church despite their intertribal diversity. They take care of one another and meet one another's needs when babies are born or someone gets sick. Martha cites this caregiving as one of the fruits of the women's Bible study.

Reconciliation, love, and evangelism are also fruits of the Bible study. Two Kenyan neighbors were enemies. One of the ladies, who was flirting with both Christianity and Islam, started coming to the church's Bible study. Her life was transformed by the Word. She went looking for her neighbor and apologized for not being good to her. Now they are both Christians and attend the Bible study together. This is only one example of the transformative power of a Bible study focused on the truth of the Word.

Discipling

As the women at Kibera know, those who are very different can find unity around the Word of God. Consider two women at an English-speaking church in the Middle East, one American and one Japanese. Kim is an older woman with four children, and Yuri is a younger, recently married woman. On the outside they had very little in common, but they began to share their joys and sorrows and to counsel one another from the Word of God. They prayed together, confessed their sins to one another, and built each other up in the faith. As they grew, they began leading a small-group Bible study together, and both began discipling other women. Their love for Christ and for one another touched the lives of many women and served as a catalyst for many others to meet together for prayer and accountability. What a multiplication of ministry!

Even women with the same first language and skin color come from many different family backgrounds, have different felt needs, and deal with different circumstances in life. Applying the universal truth of the Word of God to our varying stages of life and circumstances brings unity and spiritual growth.

Biblical Hospitality

The ancient Near Eastern context of the Bible heavily emphasized hospitality. One of the qualifications of elders, the leaders of the church, is to be hospitable (1 Tim. 3:2; Titus 1:8). Paul, Peter, and the writer of Hebrews all command hospitality (Rom. 12:13; Heb. 13:2; 1 Pet. 4:9). Peter gives a full view of the goal and outcome of hospitality: "Above all, keep loving one another earnestly, since love covers a multitude of sins. Show hospitality to one another without grumbling. As each has received a gift, use it to serve one another, as good stewards of God's varied grace . . . in order that in everything God may be glorified through Jesus Christ" (1 Pet. 4:8–11). In these verses, Peter describes the church as a living organism, loving and serving one another in spiritual and practical ways that magnify Jesus Christ and show God's grace as the giver of all gifts. Hospitality in the church brings life, love, and relationship to the members and is the perfect vehicle to sow seeds of the Word of God, both within and across the cultures of the world.

Dubai, a city in the United Arab Emirates, where I live, is an international haven in the Middle East. Most residents here come from somewhere else. Our church is comprised of expatriates from all over the world, so hospitality is crucial. We love to meet in each other's homes, enjoy a monthly church-wide meal together, prepare meals for members who are sick or moving residence or having new babies, and enjoy fellowship at the biannual church picnics. Our diversity is highlighted in our gatherings around food. The smell of Adiam's roasting coffee beans from Ethiopia wafts through the air, while Darly's flavorful biryani is served, and Etienne puts on a South African Braai. In all these things, we endeavor to speak of Christ and provide honey from the Word as well as from our kitchens.

Hospitality flows among the whole congregation, of course, but in women's gatherings it creates a unique intimacy and opportunity to share lives and eventually families that, apart from Christ, might never blend in unity. One of the most enjoyable things we do is to host wedding and baby showers for our members. Bethany, an American who grew up in Djibouti, does a spectacular job of decorating a room in the church building and organizing refreshments. One of the older women in the church gives a devotional from the Scriptures. In this way, our fellowship and love for one another is not just about the upcoming excitement of the wedding or birth but an occasion to rejoice together in the Word and to celebrate the occasion in light of its truth.

As we feed one another and give one another rest, we can feed on the Word together. We can sow seeds that grow and build up the church in encouragement, creating more life and more love that magnify Jesus Christ because he loved us first. His is the ultimate display of hospitality. He invited us in while we were still sinners, his enemies. We were dead in our transgressions and sins, but he fed us with the bread of life—his body that was broken for us—and brought us to life. He bids us to rest in him as we now show self-sacrificial hospitality to others.

Word-Centered Outreach

Satan has infiltrated all cultures and blinded the world to the truth of the gospel (2 Cor. 4:4). He has deceptively crafted false religions and ways of life to oppose God. None of them is neutral. Each false religion involves a worldview that actively works against the gospel, convincing unbelievers of their ability to please the ultimate force in the universe (which, in the case of an atheist, she may think is herself). These worldviews run deep in cultures, entrapping and enslaving adherents. In Eastern cultures, and increasingly in Western cultures, a short presentation of who Jesus is and what he has done is usually not enough to unpack a lifetime shaped by a false worldview.

We must take women to the Scriptures to see for themselves who Jesus truly is. Paul called them "the sacred writings, which are able to make you wise for salvation through faith in Christ Jesus" (2 Tim. 3:15). Becky Valdez testifies to the power of the Scriptures to change her whole view of the world:

> I was raised as a Catholic in Mexico. It was obvious to me that we were Christians and other forms of Christianity were sects; at least that is what the nuns at school taught us. When I grew older I felt something was missing. With all the religious rituals, I came to realize I did not have Jesus in my life. Then I was invited to a Bible study that a Christian friend was leading. I decided to give it a try. I felt a strong desire to know God better and get closer to him. It was then, when I started to read the Bible, that everything became so clear to me—who God was and who I really was—and that brought me to the cross of Jesus and his saving power. I understood why Jesus had to die for my sins, and I experienced God's forgiveness and love in the person

of Christ. For the first time I had a deep, intimate relationship with the Savior that I never had before, and I felt a love for him that I never knew before. That was the start of a life transformation that still to this day goes on.

Becky, who now teaches the Bible to other women, was previously blinded by ritual, but the blinders fell off when she started reading the Bible. Rituals and law keeping also blind the adherents of Islam. Islam is a religion set up in direct opposition to Christ. The Muslim holy book, the Koran, teaches that God does not have a son. Islam insists that Jesus did not die on the cross, but he was taken off the cross and up to heaven while his body was replaced by a criminal. It takes a lot of unpacking to explain the gospel to a Muslim. But we don't have to be experts in Islam to share the gospel with our Islamic friends. We need to get them reading the Bible.

One Muslim woman, Salima, became interested in Christianity. Her culture's taboo against reading the Bible intrigued her, so she asked two friends who had been open about their Christian faith to teach her about Christianity. These two friends got her a Bible and began reading through the Gospel of Mark with her, encouraging her to read on her own also. When she read about Jesus calming the wind and the waves, she said, "Well, of course, he created the wind and the waves, so he could calm them." The living Word began to open Salima's eyes to the truth about Jesus, and she saw his call on her life. Salima's father's family were devout Muslims from Yemen. As a child, Salima had her jaw broken by an uncle for asking a question about Islam. However, when she read Mark 8:35, "For whoever would save his life will lose it, but whoever loses his life for my sake and the gospel's will save it," she understood the application to her life. Salima said, "I may have to give up my life to follow Jesus, but it is worth it because I will have peace with God."

No matter what our background, we need to be brought to the Scriptures. Jenny, a pastor's wife in the Middle East, began meeting with a woman who was newly attending her church, a successful businesswoman from the Philippines who had grown up going to church. She insisted she was a good person and had no need to repent of her sins; she was doing a fine job of working her way to God. Through patient conversation facilitated by reading the Scriptures, Jenny watched as the woman's eyes were opened to her sinful heart's rebellion against God. The woman came to realize she had done nothing to deserve God's favor but instead was deserving of punishment and death. She repented and believed. The Holy Spirit and the Word did the work, and Jenny got to watch while God drew this precious woman to himself.

Satan has worked hard to keep people all over the world from "seeing the light of the gospel of the glory of Christ, who is the image of God" (2 Cor. 4:4). But "by the open statement of the truth" (2 Cor. 4:2), which is God's Word, we women can proclaim that Jesus Christ is Lord and see our friends' eyes opened to "the light of the knowledge of the glory of God in the face of Jesus Christ" (2 Cor. 4:6). The beauty of the gospel is that it is universal. Regardless of background, language, or culture, we are all sinners in need of a Savior. And the same amazing message offers salvation to all.

What a privilege it is to do ministry among women! We can have confidence in God's Word and be bold to invite women into it through ministries that are Bible-saturated—ministries like Kabwata Baptist Church in Lusaka, Zambia. The women of Kabwata engage in Bible study, hospitality, evangelism, and mentoring. With a variety of women of different ages and stages of life, the ministry thrives under the Word of God. The senior pastor's wife, Felistas, says, "The elders train leaders through the preached word and through Bible studies. Older women have a deliberate policy of training younger ladies and praying together for leaders. God's Word is shared for salvation and sanctification of ladies. God's

Word is shared whenever and wherever we do ladies' activities so that ladies are governed by the Word of God." The vigor, confidence, and intentionality of this voice of a sister from Zambia can challenge all of us, wherever we minister.

CLARITY ABOUT GOD'S GLORIOUS GOSPEL

In 1 Corinthians 15:3–4 Paul writes: "For I delivered to you as of first importance what I also received: that Christ died for our sins in accordance with the Scriptures, that he was buried, that he was raised on the third day in accordance with the Scriptures." This is the gospel, the matter of first importance. Women engaged in God-glorifying ministry are caught up in the gospel message, and that message motivates and informs their lives and ministry. It is the gospel that saves us, and it is the gospel that sustains us. Naomi, from Kenya, shares how a deeper knowledge of the gospel transformed her life:

> I became a believer in a small charismatic church in Northern Jakarta, Indonesia, a few months after we arrived there. God called me (not that I knew this truth then—I thought I had just decided it was time) in the midst of an emotional turmoil that can come with a move to a new culture. I grew up in church and understood sin then as something bad that I would do sometimes. I did not know that mine was a sinful nature, bound and shackled without hope apart from Christ. And so as a young believer this hazy truth played into how I tried to live out my new life—by being good. And I was frustrated most of the time. I felt like I was hanging in there, not sure when my efforts would fail. I was afraid I would not be able to hold onto my salvation to the end. But I loved the Word, and the church in Jakarta encouraged us to read the Word.
>
> We moved again and started attending a gospel-centered church. I must say that even by this time I had not truly grasped

what salvation by grace really meant. And over the years at my church, as the whole truth has been faithfully broken down (word, verse, chapter, and book by book), the majestic truth and unity in the redemptive story in the Bible has become clear—Genesis makes sense in Revelation and vice versa (as is the case with all the other books). For how can anyone understand John 3:16 without understanding Genesis 3 and so on? The gospel is the main point, not anyone's point of view. And when the gospel is at the center of the church, hearts are awakened to the only truth that sets mankind free.

It is in knowing this truth that I can now tell anyone boldly about the hope I have in Christ. I am no longer hanging in there, but I am alive because I know Christ sustains me by his name. I am able to love others in the body (not perfectly) because he loved the unlovable me and included me in this body, the church for which he died. It is because of this good and sound teaching that I am able to discern unsound doctrine and teaching.

And the effects are not on me alone, but this truth reverberates among other saints in the church too. As I witness the ladies at the women's Bible study love one another, I am amazed to see them have honest, genuine conversations about the Word, teaching and admonishing one another. This I have greatly benefitted from. I am amazed at the gospel-centered conversations that I have heard many hours after the study and how I have left those conversations feeling so encouraged for the good fight. This is what the true gospel generates.

Naomi gained a fuller understanding of the majesty and unity of the redemptive storyline of the Bible, and this enabled her to fight sin, love others, and share the gospel boldly. This is wonderful fruit of a gospel-centered ministry.

How can women doing ministry keep the gospel at the forefront? We must be intentional. When we teach we should make it a point always to explain the gospel message and how it relates to the passage being taught. We set each passage in its overall biblical context. We don't shy away from doctrine—especially the doctrines of grace that hold up Jesus Christ as having taken the wrath of God for hopeless sinners. We prayerfully depend on the Spirit of the risen Christ to guide our understanding of his Word. When we hold each other accountable or pray for one another, we keep in mind that we are great sinners but have a greater God. When we counsel each other through difficult times, we remind each other of the glory that awaits us in Christ Jesus. The gospel is proclaimed at social events, and women are encouraged to share the gospel with family, neighbors, and friends. The whole ministry should reverberate with the message that God saves undeserved sinners through his Son, Jesus.

Padmini leads a Bible study of Indian women in her church and describes her ministry as "encouraging and supporting the spiritual growth of women and leading them to view their daily lives keeping the gospel message at the center." She and the other women in her church are intentional about the centrality of the gospel. And then there's Sheena, another great example of a gospel-centered woman. Sheena leads a women's ministry in her church in the country of Oman, where there are many government restrictions. They can't hold meetings in homes or invite Muslims to church, and proselytization is illegal. This makes their focus on the gospel even more vital to the ministry. Sheena insists, "God is not limited by government restrictions. We regularly teach [women] how to share the gospel in a simple and clear way. We encourage them to build relationships with other ladies through friends of their kids, the teachers who teach them, household help, neighbors, and people they meet through weekly activities like sports, the gym, etc."

How does a ministry lose the gospel? Typically this occurs when leaders water it down to make it more palatable in an effort to bring more people in. They don't guard the good deposit (2 Tim. 1:14). They let other, perhaps seemingly more positive, or practical, or comforting ideas take precedence over Christ crucified as they work to meet people's felt needs. Sadly, this gospel diminution is evident all over the world. Churches in India practice syncretism with Hinduism and Islam. The false gospel of prosperity has taken over many churches in Africa and the Far East. And the gospel is largely absent, to be found only occasionally in the liturgy, in high churches all over Europe. Just like every ministry in the church, women's ministries must guard the good deposit and keep the gospel the matter of first import. The gospel should be the bright red thread that runs through all teaching, hospitality, and fellowship. This thread not only should stand out and decorate every church activity and good work but should hold everything together. Without it, ministry falls apart and becomes fruitless. To keep the gospel thread running through all of ministry, we must celebrate the true gospel, and we must guard against the following substitutes.

What the Gospel Is Not

First, the gospel is not just talking about God and what he has done in our lives. We should enjoy talking about how much God has done for us, and our testimonies can encourage one another and sow seeds in the hearts of unbelievers. However, they can leave our friends thinking, "I'm glad she's found something that works for her, but that has nothing to do with my life." Testimonies about God's work in our lives are not enough. Only the gospel—the objective truth about God sending his only Son, Jesus, to pay the penalty for the sin of anyone who repents and believes in him—saves.

Second, the gospel is not just talking about how much we like Jesus. Muslims and Hindus also like Jesus. Miriam, a Muslim Emirati, insists that Muslims highly esteem Jesus and believe he is coming back to finish his work of judgment. Muslims regard Jesus as a great prophet but not as God. Priya, a former Hindu from India, leads a book study with the women of her church. She says, "Hindus are happy to add Jesus to their pantheon of gods. I encourage our women to push further when sharing the gospel and talk about the exclusivity of Christ." Even many atheists like Jesus and think he was a good guy. Neither the religious nor the irreligious have a problem with Jesus generally. The problem they have is with the biblical view of Jesus being the only way to right relationship with God. Jesus said, "I am the way, and the truth, and the life. No one comes to the Father except through me" (John 14:6). Jesus is the unique Son of God, who alone can deliver people from judgment. We must hold up this exclusivity to explain who Jesus truly is and what he has done. Otherwise, we aren't telling people the way to be saved. We aren't really telling them the gospel.

Third, the gospel is not a means to living the good life. Many churches and even missionaries hold up this view of Christianity because it is enticing to a hurting world. "Become a Christian, and you will be blessed materially: You will be healthy, wealthy, and happy in your relationships with others." It's sad when the prosperity gospel gets preached in wealthy America and Europe, but it is tragic to see it spreading through poverty-stricken populations in Africa, Iran, and China.

Mary, a Scottish missionary, was meeting with a group of Iranian women. Some had converted to Christianity and joined the Iranian church she attended, and some others were Muslim. To Mary's alarm, the Christians were trying to convince the Muslims their lives would get better if they became followers of Jesus—they would get better jobs, have better marriages, and have better health. One of the Muslim women responded, "Maybe my life would be better for a while. But what about when things go wrong, like they do in everyone's lives at times? What do I do with Jesus then?" This Muslim woman was wise. She saw through the prosperity gospel to the reality of a fallen world. Thankfully, Mary was able to build a relationship with this woman and share the true gospel with her.

Even if we don't believe Jesus came simply to make us healthy and wealthy in a world that is presently passing away, sometimes we can suggest this in our evangelism or counseling of other women. Do we counsel hurting women to pray for miracles that will take them out of their difficult situations, or do we give them the hope of a God who comforts us through trials and will never leave or forsake us? Do we encourage women to have faith that God will solve their problems and ease their pain, or do we tell women that God will use even their problems and pain to do them good and bring glory to himself? We can use difficulty in women's lives to point them to Jesus, not as the solution to their immediate felt needs but as the satisfier of their deepest need—reconciliation with a holy God.

This is especially important when reaching out in a Muslim context. We must warn Muslim women to count the cost before following Christ. They will be persecuted. They will likely lose family, security, and possibly even their lives. One Muslim friend from Somalia told me, "Westerners don't understand what it's like for us in Muslim countries. The government doesn't have to execute us if we convert. Our families will kill us while the government looks the other way." This happened recently in Saudi Arabia, where the father of a sixteen-year-old girl cut out her tongue and killed her for becoming a Christian. No, the gospel is not a means to living the good life in this fallen world. It is much greater and more lasting than that. And it is worth our giving up our earthly lives. We must clearly counsel women to count the cost and teach them that this world is not our home.

It's important to know what the gospel is not. It's not just God talk. It's not just that we like Jesus. It's not how to live the good life materially. The gospel is so much more. It is the message that sinners, through Jesus Christ, can be reconciled to a holy God, enabled to know him and glorify him by enjoying him forever. "For all have sinned and fall short of the glory of God, and are justified by his grace as a gift, through the redemption that is in Christ Jesus, whom God put forward as a propitiation by his blood, to be received by faith" (Rom. 3:23–25).

CONNECTION WITH THE LOCAL CHURCH

From all the peoples of the world, God is bringing together "a chosen race, a royal priesthood, a holy nation, a people for his own possession" (1 Pet. 2:9). These people make up the church, described in Revelation as "the holy city, new Jerusalem, coming down out of heaven from God, prepared as a bride adorned for her husband" (Rev. 21:2). What beautiful pictures of the church! A radiant bride in pure white. A bejeweled city where its lamp never goes out and its gates never shut. Until the day when the city comes down out of heaven, local churches will be outposts of that city, colonies of heaven. This is why Paul tells the local church at Corinth, "Strive to excel in building up the church" (1 Cor. 14:12).

There is certainly a place for parachurch organizations. On the Arabian Peninsula, a university fellowship is doing powerful work among students. Many from a variety of different religious backgrounds have come to know Christ, and those who already follow Christ are built up in the faith and spurred on to evangelize their unbelieving classmates. However, although this fellowship is parachurch, they encourage the students to be members of local churches. These students bring energy to their churches, and their churches serve and encourage them during this pivotal time of life.

Sadly, some parachurch organizations underplay the importance of the church, and this can be true of women's ministries run apart from the church. One pastor in Malaysia lamented that his members who attend an outside inductive Bible study didn't seem to have the time or interest to invest in the church. He appreciated that they were studying the Bible, but they were often too busy with the parachurch activity to engage in the local church. Each of us has a limited amount of time to divide among family, church, work, and relationships. We would all do well to ask ourselves challenging questions such as: Who am I primarily committed to? How could my resources of time and talent be more effectively used for the church? Am I cultivating knowledge about the Bible more as an individual than in the context of ongoing relationships and worship and family? Am I living a God-centered, church-oriented life, or do I just do Bible study on the side?

A healthy church is fertile soil for fruitful women's ministry, as chapter 4 has unfolded in depth. Anywhere in the world, it makes sense for women in a local church, sitting under the same preaching, to study the Bible together. They are already becoming informed and united in their theology. When a difficult question arises, they approach it from the same foundation and can check their conclusions with pastors and elders. Those elders can also provide oversight and advice about materials and leadership, as they are responsible before God to shepherd the souls of the women and the men in their congregation. In addition to individual spiritual growth, a church-based women's ministry builds up the entire church as women come to know one another intimately and form lasting bonds of friendship that overflow into relationships among families. Here is Monica, a women's Bible study leader and teacher from South Africa:

> The Lord has used his Word through gifted preachers and teachers to teach me more about his character, and that led to an increase in my love for God and his church. I think that the biggest lesson I have learned is the importance of the church as a testimony of God's truth. Being part of a community of believers who are striving to live the truths of the Word has been for me the best part of my life. My greatest joy has been to be a part of the women's ministry. Teaching and studying the Word

of God with other ladies is how we build community. We study and pray together, laugh together and, at times, cry together, but the Word of the Lord is the glue that holds the ministry together. It was through the study of God's Word that I learned to love the church.

Monica experienced joy in community that cannot be found anywhere else on earth. As she poured her time and mind into the study of God's Word in her local church, both she and the church were built up.

Commitment to the local church can also increase evangelism. When unbelievers see the church body functioning, they are drawn to the beauty of it. The church is not just a single-sex group in the same stage of life but consists of men and women of all ages, in all stages, and from varying socioeconomic groups, coming together to worship the Lord of the universe. When unbelievers see this unity based only on Christ, they see the glory of the one who is the head over all things and who was given "to the church, which is his body, the fullness of him who fills all in all" (Eph. 1:22–23).

At one of the baby showers we hosted at our church in Dubai, an expecting mom named Omolade, from Nigeria, brought along a Muslim friend of hers. Our devotional was on Deuteronomy 6. We discussed the goodness of the Lord's commands—and the fact that we really have no hope of perfectly fulfilling them—*and* the most important fact that Jesus died for sinners, so that, even when we fail to teach our children well, we have great hope in him. When Omolade's friend left the shower, she expressed her surprise at how much we, in the church, care for one another, even though we are from so many different cultural and economic backgrounds. She wanted to know more about Jesus, the one who unites us. She had heard the gospel and seen it lived out among the ladies of our church.

In John 17, the night before he goes to the cross, Jesus prays for future believers to "be one, . . . so that the world may believe that you have sent me" (John 17:20–21). He goes on to declare to his Father that the glory given to him (Jesus) has been given to believers, "that they may be one even as we are one" (v. 22). There is something uniquely powerful about unity among believers on display in the local church. If you want to see evangelism increase, and if you want to see exponential spiritual growth among women, do ministry under the authority of a local church. Remember, churches are outposts of heaven. There is so much to do in a local church: Bible study, discipling, teaching, hospitality, service, outreach. Where better to spend our time, our talents and gifts, our resources, and our lives than with true family in this outpost of our ultimate home?

PEOPLE FROM EVERY TRIBE, TONGUE, AND NATION

Dubai, in the United Arab Emirates, is not far from where Jesus commissioned his disciples to be his witnesses even "to the end of the earth" (Acts 1:8). In many ways Dubai feels like the end of the earth. Situated in the middle of the Muslim world, it is a mecca (pun intended) for unreached people groups from all over the world. While mosques appear on every corner, many Hindus, Sikhs, and Buddhists, as well as ordinary agnostics, call Dubai home.

Yes, Dubai is extraordinarily diverse, with over two hundred people groups converging on the city, but it is a far cry from a melting pot. Go to a local coffee shop and you will see Emiratis, Indians, Europeans, Africans, and East Asians. But instead of blending together, they group themselves according to race and nation. At the counter of a Starbucks, standing next to one another are two women, one European and the other a local Emirati. The European woman is wearing shorts and a midriff with spaghetti straps. She has a belt wrapped twice around her bare belly and stands in five-inch high heels. The Emirati is, of course, in the traditional dress of an *abaya*, a black robe covering the entire body, including arms and legs, and a *shayla*, a black head scarf covering every strand of hair. These ladies speak different languages and are from two different continents and vastly different cultures. Their paths cross in Dubai, but only for a moment. The ladies get their coffee, part, and go back to their tables: one full of Emirati women and the other with two European men.

The coffee shop is a snapshot of Dubai—many nations living in the same place yet isolated from one another. But the church in Dubai presents a different picture. Japanese have coffee with Persians. Filipinos show hospitality to Indians. Ghanaians pray with Americans. Bible studies are comprised of mixed groups of people from every habitable continent. My own small group has women from Nigeria, Japan, Switzerland, Turkey, Australia, Eritrea, Ireland, England, Germany, and the US. The church in Dubai is a snapshot of what God is doing all over the world. The gospel, by the power of the Holy Spirit, is going out to the ends of the earth, creating a people for God from every tribe, tongue, and nation to spread his glory and enjoy him forever. In the end, these peoples won't remain in isolation but will worship God together as his treasured possession at the marriage supper of the Lamb (Rev. 19:6–10). Until that day, women have an exciting part to play as we participate in ministry that is saturated in the Word of God, caught up in the glory of the gospel, and engaged in the life of the local church.

PART 3

ISSUES IN
WOMEN'S
MINISTRY

— 7 —

Older and Younger

Taking Titus Seriously

Susan Hunt and Kristie Anyabwile

For this chapter, we (Gloria and Kathleen) didn't want simply to theorize about the importance of older women in the church teaching and training younger women as prescribed in Titus 2. We wanted to listen in on part of the conversation. So we invited two women actively engaged in ministry to carry on a kind of public dialogue. Susan Hunt, who has spent a good deal of her life encouraging Titus 2 discipleship, first writes a letter to the younger generation. Kristie Anyabwile, representing the younger generation, follows with a letter to older women. But that's not all. The chapter concludes with a personal response from each to the other: Susan to Kristie, and finally Kristie to Susan. It's a lovely and thought-provoking dialogue about older-woman-to-younger-woman discipling relationships. Such relationships, we should clarify, are not the same as Bible study and do not replace Bible study—although they certainly will involve searching the Scriptures together in the process of sharing our lives as women. These relationships often combine with or grow naturally out of the process of Bible study. Susan calls them "Titus 2 discipleship"; Kristie calls them "mentoring relationships"; but whatever we call them, we should consider this call to make such relationships part of our lives as Christian women living in obedience to the Word. May this chapter encourage many more dialogues among generations of women in the church.

A LETTER TO THE YOUNGER WOMEN OF THE CHURCH, FROM SUSAN HUNT

I wish we could sit on my porch with a glass of iced tea and have this Titus talk. There are so many things I want to share with you, things I wish I had known at your age. Today let's talk about *why* we should take the Titus mandate seriously. Let's start with Titus 2:3–5:

> Older women likewise are to be reverent in behavior, not slanderers or slaves to much wine. They are to teach what is good, and so train the young women to love their husbands and children, to be self-controlled, pure, working at home, kind, and submissive to their own husbands, that the word of God may not be reviled.

I was in my mid-forties before I saw the wonder and beauty of this biblical imperative. As a young pastor's wife, my spiritual arrogance prevented me from valuing older women in my life. I judged their spirituality by my standards and failed to recognize their quiet, steady, decades-long obedience through times of weeping and rejoicing. I did not take Titus 2 seriously and missed one of God's rich provisions for my growth in grace. My grief over my sin and loss is eclipsed by the wonder of God's patience with, and love for, his prideful child.

It's a lovely gift that now, in my mid-seventies, I've been asked to share my Titus adventure with you. It was never a solo journey. My Titus 2 convictions and commitments were formulated in the context of a church that preaches sound doctrine. The Lord used my husband and other godly male leaders in our church, many women, and two life events to shape the trajectory of this journey.

The first event was almost thirty years ago, when I became director of women's ministry for the Presbyterian Church in America. I quickly realized there were few resources to help us navigate our way through the confusion about what women's ministry should be and do in a complementarian context, so I went to God's Word and landed on Titus 2:3–5.

Slowly the Titus idea captivated my mind, but at first I had a minimalist perspective of it. I was frantic to develop a plan to match older and younger women and check this task off my list, but as I prayed over this passage, I began to look at the whole chapter, then the whole letter, and then the whole Bible. The Westminster Larger Catechism explains, "The scriptures manifest themselves to be the word of God . . . by the consent of all the parts, and the scope of the whole, which is to give all glory to God."[1] Seeing the "scope of the whole" helped me see this particular part of God's Word with more clarity. My passion for Titus 2 intensified, and my vision expanded, as I saw this covenant family responsibility as part of the grand story of redemption. (See chapter 1 of this book.)

The redemption story began before the beginning when God chose us in Christ to be his own and to reflect his glory (Eph. 1:4, 6). Then he created man in his image: "male and female he created them" (Gen. 1:27). (See chapter 2 for a fuller discussion.)

The first woman was perfectly happy being the helper she was created to be until Satan inverted the creation order and went to her, tempting her to question and disobey God's command. When she and then her husband ate the forbidden fruit, they became covenant breakers. However, before creation the Father, the Son, and the Holy Spirit made a covenant to redeem a people, and the triune God is a covenant keeper. He did not leave them in their sin and misery. He promised that the offspring of the woman would defeat Satan (Gen. 3:15). In response to this first revelation of the covenant of grace,[2] Adam "called his wife's name Eve, because she was the mother of all living" (v. 20).

Eve means "giver of life." I don't think this redemptive calling to be a life giver is only biological. The life of Christ in us enables women to be life givers, rather than life-takers, in every relationship, circumstance, and season of life. God's grace empowers us to nurture covenant life—life based on the unfailing promises of God to us in Christ—in our homes, churches, neighborhoods, and workplaces.

The exquisite beauty of covenant life among God's people is described in the Westminster Confession of Faith, where we are taught that if we are united to Christ, we are "united to one another in love, [have] communion in each other's gifts and graces, and are obliged to the performance of such duties, public and private, as do conduce to [our] mutual good, both in the inward and outward man."[3]

Even as men and women find redemption in Christ, in a fallen world our creation purpose to live for God's glory and our redemptive calling to live covenantally are counterintuitive and countercultural. Like Cain we ask, "Am I my brother's keeper?" (Gen. 4:9). We need to be discipled in God's Word, which is exactly what Jesus commissioned his church to do (Matt. 28:18–20). Titus 2:3–5 makes this gospel commission gender specific. Some discipleship—not all, but some—is to be woman-to-woman, because one of the "all things" we are to teach is that God designed gender distinctiveness and assigned gender-specific roles. Titus 2 is so much more than a buddy system that pairs younger and older women. Titus 2 is about being our sister's keeper and discipling her to live for God's glory according to his Word. Titus 2 is one part of the church's obedience to the Great Commission. Titus 2 is about being life givers. By renewing my mind so that I saw the magnitude of this magnificent mandate, the Lord prepared me for the next step in this journey.

The second life event that influenced my Titus story was my husband's call to serve a church with a rich generational blend of godly people. Titus 2's theological hold on me became intensely personal and practical. I taught a Bible study with women older and younger than I, and I wondered: "Am I an older or a younger woman?" My passion about the Titus idea seeped into everything I taught, and we began to discuss the implications of T2D (Titus 2 discipleship).

Rather than being disappointed when older women did not take leadership, I listened to them. We asked them to share their stories, to tell us what they wish they had known at our age, and to tell us their favorite Bible verses and hymns. Soon older and younger women were getting to know, love, and learn from each other as we discussed the application of God's Word and prayed together. We came to the wonderful realization that each of us was a younger and an older woman; there was a vibrant mutuality as we learned from and nurtured the faith of one another.

Titus 2 begins, "But as for you, teach what accords with sound doctrine." Paul wrote this to Titus, the pastor. The directive for women to disciple women is given to the leaders of the church. This ministry is to take place under their oversight and in the context of sound doctrine and covenant community life, that is, where the covenantal principle of one generation declaring God's mighty acts to the next generation is practiced (Deut. 6:1–9; Pss. 145:4; 78:1–7). Paul's description of this kind of discipleship is profound and timeless:

But we were gentle among you, like a nursing mother taking care of her own children. So, being affectionately desirous of you, we were ready to share with you not only the gospel of God but also our own selves, because you had become very dear to us. (1 Thess. 2:7–8)

Covenantal discipleship is educational, relational, and transformational. Women need godly, mature women to *teach* them "what is good" according to God's Word. Women need to learn the theological basis for our creation design, our roles in the home and church, and our calling to be life givers in every role and stage of life. Women need women who will *share their lives* to train them how to apply the Word in all of life—how to love others, care for their families, cultivate community, work productively, and extend compassion according to God's Word. They need godly women who prayerfully and continually point them to the sufficiency of Scripture to *transform* them from life takers to life givers.

Titus 2:3–5 is a mothering ministry. It happens "when a woman possessing faith and spiritual maturity enters into a nurturing relationship with a younger woman in order to encourage and equip her to live for God's glory."[4] A woman does not have to be a biological mother to be a spiritual mother. Some of the most extraordinary mothers in Israel I have known are single women who never birthed a child. The call to spiritual motherhood gives them great joy and comfort.

The more women in our Bible study shared our lives with each other, the more we realized that the call to life-on-life discipleship is costly. Physical mothering is sacrificial. So is spiritual mothering. We began asking the *why* question: *Why* should a woman make this investment? Whether we want to *be* or *have* a spiritual mother, if we are motivated by guilt, self-fulfillment, or excitement about a new program in our women's ministry, we will fizzle when the relationship disappoints us. Paul gives the only reasonable reason to obey such a self-sacrificing calling:

> For the grace of God has appeared, bringing salvation for all people, . . . [for we are] waiting for our blessed hope, the appearing of the glory of our great God and Savior Jesus Christ. (Titus 2:11–13)

The gospel is the only motive that will incentivize us to lifelong obedience—Jesus appeared in grace and he will appear in glory. Between his two appearings we are to make disciples.

Paul is also quick to assure us that it is gospel power, not our persuasiveness, that will save and sanctify the women we disciple. The passage continues:

> . . . our great God and Savior Jesus Christ, who gave himself for us to redeem us from all lawlessness and to purify for himself a people for his own possession who are zealous for good works. (vv. 13–14)

Jesus is redeeming and purifying his people. The pressure is off. When and how a woman responds to my nurturing is the work of God's grace. But whether she responds or not, God will do his redeeming and purifying works in me as I share the gospel and my life with others.

This is not my story; it is the story of God's grace. My delayed response to Titus 2 was part of his sovereign plan for me, perhaps to give me a passion to urge *you* not to miss any opportunity to become a woman involved in discipleship relationships with other women.

My young friend, I may not know your face or your name, but if you trust in Christ alone for your salvation, you are my spiritual daughter because God has adopted us into his family. Paul's words to the Philippians express my thoughts about you: "I thank my God in all my remembrance of you . . . because of your partnership in the gospel. . . . And I am sure of this, that he who began a good work in you will bring it to completion at the day of Jesus Christ. It is right for me to feel this way about you all, because I hold you in my heart, for you are all partakers with me of grace" (Phil. 1:3–7).

Susan

A LETTER TO THE OLDER WOMEN OF THE CHURCH, FROM KRISTIE ANYABWILE

I begin this letter to you with a sad story. The first two older women I asked to mentor me said no. I was devastated. I knew both women pretty well. We served together in the same church and enjoyed sweet fellowship together as sisters in Christ, and they were women whom everyone referred to as "Aunt Mary" and "Mama Gracie." When you read Titus 2:3–5, their names are written all over it as models of women who were reverent, self-controlled, lovers of their husbands and children, and so on. Many women were learning from their godly lifestyle and strong faith, so I was excited about the opportunity to spend one-on-one time with them. You may ask, "If you were already learning from them, what more were you looking for?" Having been a Christian for only a couple of years, I was looking for an older woman with whom my life could be an open book. I desired someone to hold my hand as I walked out my faith and callings as a young wife and mother. I needed a spiritual mom, someone who could help teach and train me to live for the glory of God in all of life.

When I made my first request, Mama Gracie and I met at a local restaurant. Although I knew what I would order for breakfast, I nervously scanned the menu, stalling for time and praying for boldness and just the right words to express my desires. I'd prayed for God's wisdom on just whom to ask, and believed this woman could encourage my faith as a young believer in Christ and equip me to walk in a manner worthy of the Lord. I finally placed my order, put away the menu, took a deep breath, and said something like, "Mama Gracie, thanks for coming to have breakfast with me. I've been so encouraged by your faith and have been learning so much from you as I've watched you teach the toddlers in Sunday school, care for your children and grandchildren, and care for your husband. You have been a model to me in so many ways. But I know there's much more I need to learn. I've been praying for a mentor and believe the Lord directed me to you to ask if you'd consider discipling me and helping me grow in my walk with the Lord."

Silence. Awkward pause. Mama Gracie took a deep breath and said something like, "Honey [she calls everyone "Honey"], I'm honored you would make such a request of me, but I have to say no right now. I have my grandkids keeping me busy, and work." Pause. "I don't think I have time right now." Embarrassed, hurt, and trying to play it off and let her off the hook, I responded, "Well, that's okay. I understand [I didn't]. If your schedule changes in the future, you can let me know."

"I sure will, Baby" (she calls everyone "Baby").

I finished that breakfast as soon as possible and drove home in a flood of tears. In that moment I made God a promise that, by his grace, I have kept for over twenty years. I promised God that if any woman in my local church ever asked me to mentor her, I would never say no. I would find some quality time that we could spend together in a one-to-one discipling relationship, whether once a month or once a week, whether for a few weeks or months or years.

Fast-forward years later. I was in conversation with Mama Gracie, and we were talking about the need for discipleship among younger women. Mama Gracie became very quiet, and after a moment of reflection said to me, "You know, I remember when you asked me to disciple you. Honestly, I had never been asked that question before, and I didn't know how to respond. I wasn't too busy for you. I was scared because I didn't think I could do what you were asking of me. Honey, I'm sorry for how I responded to you that day." That conversation left me thinking and praying a lot about how older women could be encouraged to embrace their calling to train younger women, according to the instructions of Titus 2.

But who are the older women? At least three proposals exist in defining who should be considered "older." Some say Christian maturity marks the older woman. Others say we're all older than someone else, so, in a sense, we can all be considered older women. Some say there is an age requirement, though none dare suggest a number!

We know from Scripture that at age fifty the Levites' priestly tabernacle duties changed from manual labor to supporting the younger men who assumed those day-to-day duties (Num. 8:25–26). We know that Naomi was at least old enough to have grown sons (Ruth 1:1–4) and was apparently beyond the age and ability to remarry and have additional children (v. 12) or to do physical labor, as Ruth went alone to glean in the fields of Boaz (2:2). The Bible praises gray hair and old age (Prov. 16:31; 20:29; Isa. 46:4). Elizabeth was in her old age when she conceived, and though pregnant at the same time, she still took on the role of encourager to the younger Mary (Luke 1:36, 39–45, 56). We also know that women could not be put on church support until they were over sixty years old (1 Tim. 5:9–10).

These brief passages lead me to address this letter to women of experienced faith who are beyond the normal marriage and child-bearing years, who are eligible for retirement from daily labor, and who may have more freedom to support and train younger women. I'd like to say three things to such older women: (1) Don't let super-high expectations discourage you. (2) We need more than practical instruction. (3) Anticipate gaining more than you give.

As I write to you, my dear older sister in Christ, I want to assure you first of all that our expectations are high. I don't say that to scare you. Rather, please realize that you have wisdom and experience that can speak directly to the needs, hurts, and desires of younger women. Older women often express concern that they'll not meet the high expectations some younger women have. We can often have unrealistic, unbiblical, inflexible, self-centered expectations of older women. But this is precisely why we need you! We need to learn to root our friendships, our counsel, our knowledge, and our womanhood in the finished work of Christ on our behalf. Christ did what we could never do for ourselves. Our efforts cannot earn us any merit before him. You can add balance to our expectations, pointing us to Christ and reminding us that our hope is in him.

Let me suggest four ways our desires can go off balance and how you might help tip the scale in the other direction:

Mother figure. Some of us realize how drastically the cultural voices around us have warped our understanding of what it means to be a woman. Some of us have lacked spiritual, godly influence from our birth moms or those who raised us. We never received practical guidance on womanhood. We need to learn from you forgiveness, biblical womanhood, and how to nurture the children in our lives.

Resident theologian. Some of us want an older woman to answer all our hard questions, to school us in theology, to be our walking Bible dictionary and concordance. We need to learn from you how to seek God for ourselves and how to dig deep in God's Word for knowledge that fuels our faith in and dependence upon Christ.

Pro bono counselor/ad hoc Holy Spirit. Some of us are looking for an older woman to solve all our problems, to rain down her years of experience and wisdom, and tell us how to respond to every roadblock we face as Christians. From you, we need to learn to rely on the Holy Spirit as our counselor and to seek God in prayer and in his Word for wisdom on how to navigate the difficulties of life.

Girlfriend/social buddy. Some of us just want a friend. We want someone to chat, cook, shop, and just hang out with. From you, we need to learn that there is a friend who sticks closer than a brother (or sister). We need to understand how to have fun for the glory of God and how to live practically and wisely in a fallen world.

Second, we need more than practical instruction. Often, when we read Titus 2:1–5, we read these verses as very practical instructions the Lord hands down from pastor to older women to younger women. It is true that how we live before God and man matters, how those of us who are wives and mothers treat our husbands and children is crucial to the love, joy, and peace we share in the home. Paul teaches that faithfulness in these practical matters makes the Word of God attractive and honored—serving as evidence of the grace of God at work in us who are saved by the gospel of Christ. A wise older woman said, "The gospel empowers and compels us to live out our design, and the gospel provides the context in which the helper design makes sense."

However, if we settle for taking care of practical concerns, focusing solely on our roles and conduct, we will fail to grasp the greater redemptive purpose in our practice. We will fail to root our endeavors in the gospel. We will fail to have our character shaped by the Spirit in all of life. We will therefore diminish our calling as redeemed women of God.

As you help us to live out Titus 2:3–5, we recognize that our greatest issue is not whether women should work outside the home, for example, but whether women are demonstrating holiness by their work in or outside the home. What matters most is that the fruit of the Spirit is on display—love, self-control, purity, diligence, kindness, submission, reverence. This focus on holiness as demonstrated by the fruit of the Spirit allows for any woman—married or single—to carry out and to receive this teaching and training. We restrict the passage in an unbiblical way when we make it solely about domesticity. Titus 2 is not merely about domesticity. It's about holiness that adorns the gospel.

Finally, I would encourage you older women to anticipate gaining more than you give. As younger women, we want to learn from you. We want to be encouraged by you, equipped by you, and corrected by you (most of the time ☺). We want to be ever growing in the faith. But I would ask that you also look to see what the Lord wants you to gain from your investment in our lives. I believe that through our times together, the Lord will continue to encourage and equip you to live for his glory, even as you encourage and train us.

Through my own limited experience in mentoring ladies younger than me, the Lord has taught me many valuable lessons I may not have learned outside of those relationships. Sometimes I can feel quite inadequate in my attempts to minister to them. The Lord reminds me that I am indeed inadequate! He emboldens me to allow younger women to see not only my trials and sins but also how I respond as God brings me through them. It is through this kind of vulnerability that I learn to make my life an open book to the women I disciple. I learn to trust in God's good purposes for my own struggles and to receive his comfort for myself so I can in turn comfort others.

I often reflect on my requests of those godly older women to mentor me. Though I was disappointed with their no, I never thought they were any less godly. I recognize that many older women have not had but greatly need and desire intentional training in spiritual mothering. Much of this training comes from the regular teaching of sound doctrine in the local church by faithful pastors and elders. More could be done in local assemblies to help older women articulate the wisdom they have gleaned through years of living as women who follow Christ, so as to pass it on to the next generation. If that does not happen, younger women can continue to learn from older women at a distance. You may not have all the training and tools, but you have a life that we can watch and imitate. God was at work in my heart through the no. May he be at work in your heart to say yes.

Kristie

SUSAN'S RESPONSE TO KRISTIE'S LETTER

Dear Kristie,

Your desire for older women in your life is evidence of God's grace in you. It is a holy desire. I'm grateful for your clarity and honesty in helping us understand what younger women need and expect from older women. I'm glad we can have this conversation while our reader friends listen in.

In my previous letter I talked about *why* we should take Titus 2 seriously; now I would like for us to think about *how* we can obey this command in our churches. Mama Gracie's explanation about why she refused your request to disciple you—"I was scared because I didn't think I could do what you were asking of me"— confirms my conviction that the hesitancy of older women is not due to disinterest or willful disobedience. Usually they are scared because they have not been equipped for the calling to teach and train young women.

A woman approached me at a conference and said, "Six months ago I asked a woman in my church to disciple me. She eagerly agreed, but I have heard nothing from her. I am desperate and disappointed." My answer: "I'm so sorry, but I strongly suspect that woman is more desperate than you are. She agreed because she wants to disciple you, but she has no idea what to do. Every day she feels increasingly inadequate and guilty."

Many churches are filled with women who want to connect

across generations, but they don't know how. Other women hold to basic sound doctrine but think in unbiblical ways regarding their womanhood. Perhaps they think independence is power and so don't admit their need for a spiritual mother, even to themselves. And there are older women who feel they are not qualified to speak into the lives of younger women. Local churches should give prayerful thought to developing a strategy to teach the biblical reason for Titus 2 discipleship, equip women for this calling, and help connect them with one another.

The need for this kind of discipleship was underscored for me when a college woman asked, "How can I possibly think biblically about my womanhood when I am constantly told that independence is power, that I determine my own destiny, and that gender is just a social construct?" I reminded her of Titus 2 and encouraged her to ask godly women in her church to disciple her in biblical principles of womanhood as a counterpoint to the world's view of gender. But her question unnerved me because I wondered if her church is equipping women for this calling.

I'm not suggesting that womanhood is the only topic older women need to teach younger women, but I am saying that *not* teaching the goodness of gender leaves women vulnerable to some of the most potent attacks on God's Word in today's culture.

Kristie, for a long time I spiritually mothered women, but I was not fruitful in equipping other women to do the same. Hearing my stories of what I did simply did not transfer to their lives. Then, as the Titus imperative took root in the minds and hearts of women in our Bible study, the women's ministry wanted to extend this reach beyond the Bible study. We developed a small-group Titus 2 discipleship model,[5] and over time a large percentage of women were involved. Covenant life became strong and sweet among the women and spilled out to the whole church. Discipleship became a way of life for women. Here are some of the benefits we discovered:

- When we recruit women to be spiritual mothers, not teachers, and promise training and ongoing support, we have no shortage of volunteers.

- A leader does not have to be the oldest woman in the group, but we ask older women to participate and be a part of a group. Leaders are trained to draw on the wisdom of these women so that we reap the blessings of their life experiences.

- There is built-in accountability. Leaders are approved by the elders, trained, given an approved curriculum, and supported through e-mail and occasional meetings where they share ideas and challenges.

- The ministry is sustainable. A coordinating committee makes needed adjustments if a leader or group members have to drop out.

- This model is adaptable, so it is easily transferable to other churches.

- More spontaneous, one-on-one relationships develop because women know how to be spiritual mothers.

As more women went through this T2D ministry, it spread to our teens and younger girls. Some women now disciple teen girls[6] and some teach elementary-age girls about God's creation design and redemptive calling. *Spiritual mother, helper,* and *life-giver* are part of the language of our church.

Of course, this small-group model did not originate with us. It is the way Jesus discipled his disciples.

There is no formula for a women's discipleship ministry. Titus 2 relationships may be formal or informal, occasional or scheduled, but unless there is an intentional effort to make Titus 2 a philosophical framework for discipling women, it is unlikely that it will become part of the culture of a church.

The mother of a young woman in our church attended one of our women's ministry events and observed, "In my church women are separated by ages. Here older and younger women, even teen girls, seem to know and love one another. How does this happen?" The daughter smiled and said, "This did not just happen. We are intentional. We take Titus 2 seriously."

Kristie, I pray that our conversation will inspire churches to equip older and younger women for the high calling of living and giving the legacy of redeemed womanhood. Much is at stake—when women obey Titus 2, God's Word will not be "reviled" (v. 5). I love you, Kristie, and I love your generation. My expectations for you are high because God "is able to do far more abundantly than all that we ask or think, according to the power at work within us" (Eph. 3:20). May we know the blessing of Paul's benediction: "To him be glory in the church and in Christ Jesus throughout all generations, forever and ever. Amen" (Eph. 3:21).

Susan

KRISTIE'S RESPONSE TO SUSAN'S LETTER

Dear Susan,

As I read your letter, my heart shouted yes! and amen! to all you said. Your years of soaking in God's Word, thinking deeply and passionately about biblical womanhood and Titus 2 discipleship, demonstrate the fruit of having been taught sound doctrine by faithful pastors who invested in your life spiritually so that you could help pass it along to the next generation.

As a younger woman transitioning to older-woman status, I am all the more certain that I need to be continuously steeped in God's Word if I'm ever to minister to my own heart or the hearts of others. My fear of theology was actually a fear of God's Word, evidence that I lacked confidence in the sufficiency of the Word for all aspects of my life. I understand the fear and anxiety that some older women experience in personal discipleship. I feel my own inadequacy, but the Lord reminds me that when I am weak, then I am strong by his strength.

I need to be discipled. I know that sin has marred God's good design of womanhood, singleness, marriage, child-rearing, and every situation we are faced with as women. Too often our lives are conformed more to the world than to the image of Christ. We must present our bodies as a living sacrifice, not perfect, but perfected through the blood of Christ, so that we might be transformed by the renewal of our minds to discern God's good and perfect will (Rom. 12:1–2). So many struggles I faced earlier in my Christian life have been occasions to praise God for his faithfulness, for his tender care and mercy, and for his trustworthy character.

I appreciated your comments on the personal benefits of Titus 2 discipleship. I would note also that Titus 2 discipleship is *personal*, *corporate*, and *global*. It is personal in our one-to-one spiritual mothering. It is corporate as an outworking of the biblical mandate for the local church, calling us to teach and admonish one another with all wisdom (Col. 3:16) so that the entire body is built up. And it is also *global*, as it commends the gospel to the non-Christian world.

First, Titus 2 discipleship is personal. For the older woman, there is the joy of nurturing and molding a younger woman and seeing her faith and maturity blossom by God's grace through your ministry. For the younger woman, there is access to regular encouragement, mentorship, discipleship, and accountability. These benefits can impact our personal lives for decades. We pray that generations of women after us—our daughters, our granddaughters, their children, and all the children being raised among God's people—will experience the blessing of this kind of ministry.

Corporately, Titus 2 discipleship creates a greater sense of trust, intimacy, and unity among the women of the church. Accountability broadens. Social circles expand within the church and minimize the formation of cliques. Women have greater opportunity to get to know each other better. These kinds of healthy corporate relationships testify to our kinship as sisters in Christ (1 Thess. 4:11); provide a sphere for living out the "one anothers" in Scripture (John 13:34; Rom. 12:10; Eph. 4:32; Col. 3:13); set forth a model for the next generation (1 Cor. 11:1); encourage the body (1 Thess. 5:11); produce spiritual growth (Phil. 3:12–17); and promote repentance and confession (James 5:16). These corporate benefits are not limited to women but mark the spiritual discipleship of all Christians as we care for one another in the body.

Discipleship among women also serves as a Christian witness to a watching, unbelieving world. The world really is watching us. They call us hypocrites. They see strife and division and turmoil among God's people. Why do they see these things? Because they don't see love. Discipleship happens when love puts on shoes. Christ states clearly that "just as I have loved you, you also are to love one another. By this *all people will know that you are my disciples, if you have love for one another*" (John 13:34–35). This is crucial. As we love one another by intentional mothering/mentoring/discipleship, the world sees and is drawn to that love. They've been longing for it all along. Now they want this same love for themselves, and we can offer it to them in the gospel.

Our discipling relationships are ultimately an evangelism catalyst. We are commanded not only to *be* disciples but also to *make* disciples. Disciples are made when the good news of Christ's atoning work is made clear, the Holy Spirit invades people's hearts, and God saves them from their sin and his judgment and for his eternal praise and glory.

Titus 2 discipleship should spark our zeal for evangelism in several ways. First, our discipleship should be gospel centered, causing us to be more gospel focused in every relationship, including with those who are not yet Christians. Too often in my own discipleship, I can assume the gospel and weaken the effectiveness of both my discipleship and my evangelism. We don't just believe the gospel at a point in time. We also live out the gospel daily. The gospel is the power of God unto salvation, and the gospel also teaches us to live soberly and uprightly as we wait for the sure and swift return of our Savior. I have greater confidence in evangelism when I see from personal experience the effect of the gospel in my own life and the lives of those I disciple or by whom I am discipled.

Second, our discipleship should be fueled by our love for one another and ignite our love for the lost and a desire to see them come to faith in Christ. Again, the world will know that we are truly Christ's by our love for one another (John 13:34–35; 1 John 4:7–11). Matthew Henry states it beautifully: "Before Christ left the disciples, he would give them a new commandment. They were to love each other for Christ's sake, and according to his example, seeking what might benefit others, and promoting the cause of the gospel, as one body, animated by one soul."[7]

Third, vibrant biblical discipleship should inspire us to grow in the grace and knowledge of Christ and embolden us to speak God's truth to those who have not yet become Christians. Our love for Christ and hunger for his Word and all the truth it contains should deepen as we spend time together as spiritual mothers and daughters. We are then more equipped to answer questions, provoke Godward thoughts, and guide unbelievers as the Spirit draws them to saving faith in Christ.

I, too, wish we were sharing a cup of tea as we reflect on how the Lord has grown us over the years as we've endeavored to live out the instructions of Titus 2. I'm sure we would need volumes to recount all the ways we've seen the Lord use our Spirit-enabled efforts to nurture and encourage other women, and even more volumes to recount the many women who have poured their hearts into our lives. At the end of my previous letter, I acknowledged that there are many women who have not been privileged with a spiritual mother. I encouraged them to learn from an older woman at a distance.

Dear Susan, this is precisely how you have influenced my life over the years. I have watched your life from afar through your writings and speaking. Much of what I've learned in regard to spiritual mothering, women's ministry, and serving as a pastor's wife, I've learned from you. And not just you. Oh, no! The Lord has taught me to love my husband through my friend Mandy. He taught me to shepherd my children through Nadia. He taught me to prioritize God's Word in my life through Nancy. Sarah taught me to pray about everything. Kim taught me how to manage my home. Eli taught me how to be hospitable. I could go on. The point is that I've continually been learning to follow the example of older women. Some of these have been intentional one-on-one relationships. Others have been very informal. Still others have been through books, conferences, and quiet watching and learning from the pew or a Sunday school class.

As I look around the sanctuary each Sunday at my church, I see many spiritual moms and daughters worshiping side by side, meeting afterward for lunch, praying and crying together after the service, scheduling teas and lunches, and serving together in the body. I see young women growing in their faith and walk with Christ. I see older women encouraged and strengthened to persevere with joy. I pray that those reading our letters will see the same in their churches, multiplied many times over, and producing fruit that we will know only in eternity.

Kristie

— 8 —

Sexual Wholeness

Affirming Truth with Compassion

Ellen Mary Dykas

Lauren and Tia[1] came to see me at Harvest USA for different reasons, but with a similar cry for help: "How can I be free of my sexual sin and this feeling of being so ashamed and dirty?" Both women professed earnest faith in Jesus Christ as Savior and Lord. Both were involved in solid evangelical churches. Lauren was a student in a biblical counseling graduate program, and Tia and her husband had both grown up hearing the Bible taught. Sadly, neither woman had heard teaching addressing the struggles many Christian women have with sexual sin and the relational brokenness almost always associated with it. Lauren's twelve-year battle with pornography and solo sex and Tia's active sexual fantasy life due to an ongoing temptation to same-sex attraction were wreaking havoc not just in their relationship with God but in all the relationships of their lives.

Lauren desired to be married but didn't feel worthy even to entertain the idea of dating, as her secret struggles overshadowed the rest of her life. She felt isolated because no one at the weekly women's Bible study ever mentioned anything slightly connected to sexual struggles. She told me, "Every so often at church there are hushed whispers about an accountability group for men who are dealing with lust, but it's totally silent regarding the struggles we [women] are having!"

Tia expressed thankfulness for her gentle and patient husband, but her desires for women, along with her embraced homosexual fantasies, were keeping a wall between her heart and his, not only emotionally but sexually and spiritually as well. She shared how disheartened she was when, on social media, she saw posts by Christian friends promoting gay marriage. She felt hopeless to know how to engage her battle with same-sex temptation without overwhelming her husband or being swayed from obedience to God by her own brothers and sisters in Christ.

This chapter is meant to help readers understand women like Lauren and Tia and to encourage women in particular to follow the steps of Jesus Christ, our gracious redeemer, into other women's lives and struggles, bringing the hope and compassion of the gospel. The gospel is indeed at the core of everything this chapter has to say. I am addressing the context of the church, where God's people affirm by faith and teach without ceasing the good news of God's redemption of us in Jesus Christ—who died in our place on the cross, who rose from the grave, conquering death, and who will come again to judge all and to dwell with his people forever. To understand the implications of the gospel for our sexuality, we have to go back to the beginning of the Bible's story.

THE CREATOR'S INTENT AND THE DEVASTATION OF THE FALL

"The earth is the LORD's and the fullness thereof, the world and those who dwell therein," proclaims Psalm 24:1. Colossians 1:16

further explains creation's Lord in speaking of Jesus: "For by him all things were created . . . all things were created through him and for him." Our God is a loving creator with a good design for all of his creation. However, no human being since Adam and Eve experiences life in this world perfectly according to that design. As a result of the fall (Genesis 3), sin has poured devastation into every detail of creation, including our sexuality. This devastation seeps with wide-ranging impact into the lives of women, deeply affecting our experience of emotional and sexual desires and, in fact, every one of our relationships.

Let's consider four key teachings of Scripture regarding our Creator's intent for sexuality and the impact of sin upon it.[2]

1) God Is the Creator of Sexuality
(Genesis 1–2; Ps. 24:1–2; Rom. 11:36; 1 Cor. 8:5–6; Col. 1:16)

The Bible reveals God (Father, Son, and Spirit) as the creator of all things. He is a loving creator and has designed everything about us—including gender, ability to interact with others, every aspect of our bodies and of our sexuality—to function according to his design. As Creator, he has decreed *why* his design is what it is: the ultimate goal is his glory, which displays the radiance of his holiness, love, goodness, power—his whole magnificent being. Human beings are made in God's image (Gen. 1:27) to display God's glorious image. We glorify God, and we experience the beauty and sanity of his design, when we follow his Word and thereby live in a way that reveals the wisdom of his character—a character the Bible reveals as worthy of worship and obedience. God's glory overflows in goodness to his creation. God is creator *and loving Lord*, so when we seek to glorify him with our bodies and through his ordained expression of our sexuality, the good gift of his design bears good fruit in our lives. This is his amazing grace revealed to us as we commit to express ourselves within the gracious guardrails of his created intent.

2) Godly Sexuality Is a Gift for the Married
(Gen. 2:24; Eph. 5:22–35; Heb. 13:4; Song of Solomon)

God's blessed context for all sexual expression is marriage. Marriage, created and designed by God, is a lifelong, committed union of one man and one woman. Godly sexuality within marriage is a way for God to be glorified, as a husband and wife experience the joys and pleasures of his good gift through:

- Selfless loving and serving of one's spouse in the context of lifelong sexual faithfulness. This means that all sexual expression is reserved for the privacy of the relationship between husband and wife, without the intrusion of any third-party influences.

- Possible new life (babies!) conceived as a fruit of sexual union.

- A bonding experience that is nurturing to the couple and also a signpost to the union of Christ with his people, the eternal reality that all believers will enjoy.

- Shameless enjoyment of sexual, emotional, and mental pleasure, which brings glory and worship to God.

3) Godly Sexuality Is a Gift for the Unmarried
(1 Cor. 7:35; Col. 3:5; Heb. 13:4)

While the married person is called to obedience to Christ through sexual faithfulness to one spouse, the unmarried person is called to obedience to Christ through abstaining from sexual expression. In spite of numerous attempts to reinterpret Scripture to allow sexual expression outside of the marriage covenant, nowhere in the Bible do we see God blessing any kind of sexual activity outside of marriage.[3] Godly unmarried sexuality is:

- A life of abstinence from sexual activity.

- A way to live out faithful devotion to Jesus, as the unmarried state allows for a unique attending upon and service to Christ.

- A platform for a variety of rich relationships.

- An opportunity to honor marriage and keep a future (or potential) marriage bed pure. Obedience to Christ as a single can prepare a woman for faithfulness as a wife.

- A signpost to Jesus that reveals him as sufficient for abundant life and worthy of complete devotion.

4) Every Woman, Single or Married, Younger or Older, Needs the Redeemer's Help in Her Sexuality.

Tia loves her husband and *is* attracted to him, but her oneness with him is being intruded upon by her fantasies of women, which she doesn't know how to dismiss—and sometimes doesn't want to. She's hurting and feels deeply ashamed not only because these images flood her mind while she is sexually intimate with her husband but also because she finds them to be mentally comforting.

Lauren knows Jesus. She longs for a deeper peace in her relationship with her Savior, but her secret sin seems untouched by all the amazing doctrinal truths she is learning at school. Her church leaders preach, teach, and encourage her to live a gospel-centered life, but she's never grasped how Christ's death and resurrection can be applied to her pornography struggle and the lust which fuels her female heart.

What's happening in the hearts of these women? Why are these daughters of the Lord struggling so deeply in their sexuality? Their struggles can speak to all of us. Simply yet profoundly, Tia and Lauren, like all women, are experiencing the impact of the fall in their sexuality. Our desires have become disordered, and our minds need transformation. Our hearts need radical reorienting toward

Christ, who has called us to live fully for him and not ourselves. We all need help connecting the loving truth of our Redeemer with these very sensitive and personal areas of our lives; we need both the *compassion* and *challenge* of God's Word and God's people.

Women facing their sexual sin and brokenness need the *compassion* of God's Word and God's people because sexual struggles can be an extended and grueling part of the battle of faith. Patterns of sexual sin generally don't become entrenched overnight, and the road of repentance will be a process. Much like making a meal in a Crock-Pot (rather than a microwave), changing patterns of sexuality often requires a long, slow simmer in God's grace and truth. The Scriptures are meant to be eaten fully and digested deeply, among God's people and over time, as the Spirit plants those words in our hearts. Temptations and desires do not usually vanish; rather, God's children learn to do battle with them, by the Spirit and the Word, with the compassionate help of God's people.

Women who are sexual strugglers need the gracious compassion of Christ extended to them also because many of them have been sinned against sexually. In my years of ministry to women like Lauren and Tia, and so many others who are ensnared somewhere in the spectrum of sexual sin, I have learned that the majority of them were sexually abused and misused for the selfish desires of others. We all tend to respond sinfully to sin committed against us; women struggling with sexual sin are no different. This chapter focuses on the many women struggling with their own sexual sin, but of course women who have been sinned against sexually struggle in all kinds of ways that need all kinds of compassion and challenge from God's people and God's Word. As we seek to disciple women like Lauren and Tia in particular, who seek release from their own bondage to sexual sin, the compassion of Christ himself is a necessity—Christ, who waited patiently with that woman caught in adultery while all the others left, before he offered her not condemnation but a call to sin no more (John 8:1–11). Women struggling with sexual sin offer God's people an opportunity to share this Lord, a Lord God full of "steadfast love" and "abundant mercy" when we call on him to "wash" and "cleanse" us (Ps. 51:1–2).

Women battling against patterns of sexual sin also need the *challenge* of God's Word and God's people, because so much is at stake! God, the loving creator of women, has designed us to flourish as we submit ourselves as living sacrifices to our holy king, Jesus. God refuses to share his glory with our idols (Isa. 42:8); he is passionate to rescue us from the false gods we pursue, which we think give us life but instead deliver disorder and death. The Lord God has good works prepared for us to extend his kingdom and to spread his love to a broken world. *This challenge isn't about getting women happier or busy in ministry.* The challenge is to be transformed into the image of Christ. Jesus rescues us from ourselves and our sin, transferring us into his kingdom so that we may be wholehearted lovers of God, worshiping him alone and participating in his mission to make disciples of all the nations (Matt. 28:18–19; Eph. 5:1–2; Col. 1:13).

THE NEED FOR DISCIPLESHIP, NOT JUST DOCTRINE

Where do we start with Lauren and Tia? Should we target their sin first or their identity in Christ? Do we initially focus Lauren on being content in her singleness and help Tia to understand what marital sexual intimacy is supposed to look like? Should we forget about their disordered sexuality and immerse them in a study of biblical womanhood? Do we really need to consider their back-story and how they were sinned against, or should we encourage them to forget what is behind them and cling to the promises of God for today?

Lauren and Tia *do* need help in all the above areas, but not only in these areas. What they have been lacking and are desperately hungry for is *targeted discipleship regarding how life in Christ connects to their struggles with sexual sin.* They need help to understand the deeper heart issues that are compelling them toward these specific sins. They need to learn, from God's Word and God's people, how Jesus gives us everything we need for life and godliness (2 Pet. 1:3–4).

Wise discipleship of women who are battling sexual sin will involve knowing them specifically in their sin struggles and then bringing the gospel specifically to their struggles as we connect them to a Savior who sees their actions and their hearts, who knows them intimately, and who in his compassion loves them enough to pursue them relentlessly. Let's consider these elements of discipleship through a story of the ministry of Jesus to a hurting woman:

> Now he was teaching in one of the synagogues on the Sabbath. And behold, there was a woman who had had a disabling spirit for eighteen years. She was bent over and could not fully straighten herself. When Jesus saw her, he called her over and said to her, "Woman, you are freed from your disability." And he laid his hands on her, and immediately she was made straight, and she glorified God. But the ruler of the synagogue, indignant because Jesus had healed on the Sabbath, said to the people, "There are six days in which work ought to be done. Come on those days and be healed, and not on the Sabbath day." Then the Lord answered him, "You hypocrites! Does not each of you on the Sabbath untie his ox or his donkey from the manger and lead it away to water it? And ought not this woman, a daughter of Abraham whom Satan bound for eighteen years, be loosed from this bond on the Sabbath day?" As he said these things, all his adversaries were put to shame, and all the people rejoiced at all the glorious things that were done by him. (Luke 13:10–17)

There's a lot happening in this passage. Jesus is seeking to illustrate what the Sabbath is really for: *God's lovingkindness experienced by his people*, and specifically here by this marginalized woman. He is ultimately seeking to show who he is and why he came; he is the deliverer come to release people from Satan's bonds (v. 16).

Let's get the scene. The synagogue was the religious gathering place, and Jesus was the teacher that day. As was the custom, only men were allowed to interact with and sit near the teacher. Women were allowed to come to the synagogue but were kept separate from the men. This bent-over woman would have been listening from a balcony or perhaps somewhere along the periphery of the room, behind a veil or other barrier. She was listening and watching from a distance, with a crowd of men between her and the Lord. Jesus beautifully puts this nameless woman's brokenness on display as he makes her the centerpiece of his display of compassionate love.

Lauren and Tia have a lot in common with this bent-over woman. They don't have a physically bent state but a spiritual, emotional, and sexual one. They too feel as if they live on the margins of their Christian communities: unknown, bent over in secret sin, weighed down under the shame of their struggles, and with perceived barriers between them and Jesus. They don't know how to receive the freedom, healing, and change they so deeply long for.

Let's seek first to know Lauren and Tia and their specific struggles through the experiences of this precious nameless woman whom Jesus loved.

KNOWING A BENT WOMAN

First, *the woman in Luke 13 is bent over and in bondage.* She had lived this way for eighteen years, bent over in pain, shuffling around, probably unable to perform daily activities without incredible struggle. In her case (and this is not always the case with physical ills), this agonizing physical bondage evidenced a spiritual bondage: this woman had a "disabling spirit," and Jesus refers to her as bound by Satan. What a vivid picture the bent body of this woman offers—a picture of the bondage in which every person lives, apart from Christ.

"Bent" implies a state in which desired uprightness has been lost and needs to be restored. This is our natural state without Christ, in bondage to sin. And so God sent his Son to deliver us. As the apostle Paul writes to the Colossians: "He has delivered us from the domain of darkness and transferred us to the kingdom of his beloved Son, in whom we have redemption, the forgiveness of sins" (1:13–14). However, even after the deliverance of salvation, believers through the power of the Spirit must learn (and often struggle) to live standing up straight in the sense of holy, healthy relationships, including the aspect of sexuality. Even while celebrating the Colossians' deliverance, Paul wrote urging them: "As you received Christ Jesus the Lord, so walk in him," and, "Put to death therefore what is earthly in you: sexual immorality, impurity . . ." (2:6; 3:5).

Sexual bondage is a persistent kind of *bentness*. Lauren learned as a teenager to use pornography and masturbation as quick ways to soothe her emotional pain. But the effect never lasted long. The physical and emotional release would soon give way to the inevitable feelings of discontent and pain that she'd felt for so long. And so she would try again, and the habits of bentness became ingrained.

Second, *the woman in Luke 13 is ostracized and judged.* Religious leaders during the time of Christ were often legalistic and judgmental: if you were suffering, it was likely due to your sin. Among the first people I got to know through Harvest USA was a forty-year-old woman who came for help. God had been moving powerfully in her heart after more than two decades of sexual promiscuity. She shared how, as a nineteen-year-old, she had been active in her church and a faithful member of the worship team. At that time, she'd finally mustered up the courage to share something with her pastor: since her early teens she had had feelings for other girls and was confused and scared by these feelings. She had not acted upon her desires but needed counsel in knowing what to do about them. "Can you help me, Pastor and pray for me? I don't know what to do with this." He responded, "We really don't have anything for you here, and you need to step down immediately from ministry involvement." And step down she did. She stepped down and out—out of the church into the open arms of people who accepted her nonjudgmentally: the lesbian community. The pastor's unloving judgment and rejection of her pain did not cause her to respond the way she did, but his response influenced her to reach out to others who would not push her away.

Before marrying, Tia shared with her husband about her past relationships with women. She shared as well her experience of being sexually abused by her pastor's son and raped by her boss at age sixteen. In the aftermath of these traumatic experiences, the desires she had for women seemed even more appealing. She thought she'd give it a try and began to date girls. She had heard the jokes and harsh condemnation in her church community about gay-identified people, so she learned how to keep her situation covered up. Now, years later, desperately seeking to follow Christ, she's even more confused: whereas the judgment pendulum once swung against homosexuality, it seems to be swinging presently against those who do not affirm it. For Tia, it seems that her same-sex fantasies will be judged by some as the worst sin, and others will judge her for not just going for it, simply following her desires. She feels very alone and misunderstood.

Third, *the woman in Luke 13 is shamed by the religious leaders.* When the ruler of the synagogue immediately protests this Sabbath healing, right in the presence of the woman who has been healed Jesus asks why the religious leaders would untie and water their animal on the Sabbath but would not loose from her bonds this suffering "daughter of Abraham." Wow! These religious leaders have basically been communicating that she wasn't as important as a donkey. This bent woman has been publicly shamed by those who had the responsibility to care for her. Of course, Jesus in accusing the leaders is actually putting *them* to shame here (v. 17) and taking away the woman's long-suffered shame.

Unlike physical bentness, which is visible, sexual brokenness often remains hidden, which actually deepens the shame of women who struggle in this way. When Lauren came to meet with me for the first time, like most women I talk with she was extremely nervous. I knew that she was an outgoing, winsome leader on her campus, but her secret had never been spoken out loud or shared with anyone. Like so many women who have confessed their sexual sin to me, tears and ache flooded out with her words as the inward pressure of keeping her secret was finally released. Shame was diffused as sin was brought out into the light with a Christian sister. She wept as she shared that she'd never heard a sermon illustration or any lectures in her biblical counseling classes that even hinted at the possibility of women being porn addicts too. She'd believed shame's lie: that her very person was muck and gunk. For years, this internal sense of shame convinced Lauren to resolve even more passionately to keep her struggle a deeply hidden secret. She was living out Proverbs 28:13a: "Whoever conceals his transgressions will not prosper."

Fourth, *the woman in Luke 13 feels captive to her body.* This woman was severely limited by her bent body, captive with no hope for freedom unless God miraculously healed and freed her from the disabling spirit. Her captivity to her disordered body gives us a way to understand the enslavement that sin has over our hearts unless our Savior saves, frees, and heals us. Paul's cry in Romans 7:24, "Wretched man that I am! Who will deliver me from this body of death?" is being echoed by many women asking this question regarding their sin of a sexual nature. They need Paul's answer to this painful cry, found in his joyful proclamation in verse 25: "Thanks be

to God through Jesus Christ our Lord!" They know they are serving
self and long to serve Christ, but they need targeted discipleship to
help them connect the truth of Romans 7:24 to that of Romans 7:25.

Many women who have been in homosexual relationships, and
perhaps even embraced a gay identity, battle hard to believe that
there is another way to live as a woman. Generally their relational
history will include a pattern of codependent (or co-idolatrous)
attachments, emotionally intoxicating relationships with women.
This is all that many of them have ever known by way of meaningful, loving, intimate connection with others. Is it truly possible to
break free and grow in godly, healthy friendships, to become *unbent*
in this area—perhaps to live in joyful singleness and perhaps to live
in joyful marriage to a man?

This was the cry of Tia's heart: "Will I ever be able to have sex
with my husband without images of women filling my mind? I feel
so dirty and so sad for him that when he is sharing himself with me,
and so longing for my full-hearted love in response, I just can't give
it. I'm divided and feel like a freak." Tia, like Lauren, knows she is
living in an unhealthy state spiritually, emotionally, and sexually.
Both feel somewhat like the woman in Luke 13, seeing Jesus from a
distance and hearing his voice. But how do they draw near to him?
How do they take the grace-filled truths of the gospel and apply
them to these areas of secret bentness? How can they see Christ
clearly through the fog of their pain and shame?

MINISTERING TO BENT WOMEN

1) Looking to Jesus, God with Us

The first and foremost ingredient of ministry to women bent with
sexual sin is the first and foremost ingredient of ministry to anyone,
any time. It is looking to Jesus, God with us. In this scene from
Luke, Jesus went to the synagogue to teach. But Jesus is more than
a teacher who presents truths about God. Jesus is our temple (John

2:21), the holy place where sin is atoned for and where God and his people meet. Jesus is the embodiment of the cry of God's heart: "And they shall be my people, and I will be their God" (Ezek. 11:20). Jesus is much more than a teacher or spiritual leader in a synagogue. The Son of God came into this sinful world; he died, he rose again, conquering sin and death, and he ascended into heaven—but he is not distant. Through his Spirit he has now come to make his home in us, his people.[4] The risen Christ is our indwelling Lord who has come near to the brokenhearted—into our very hearts.

Sexually broken women in our churches and communities need first of all to be called to Jesus, who is God with us. Many who assume they are believers may actually need to put their faith for the first time in this Redeemer who has come to us in our sin, died for that sin, and called us like he called the bent woman in Luke 13: "Woman, you are freed" (v. 12). Many who belong to Christ need the kind of personal discipleship that, with compassion and challenge, helps them draw near to the Savior, who has drawn near to us. Many need to hear us fellow sinners who have drawn near and found grace to help in time of need tell our stories of Christ's sufficiency. It is the gospel, the good news of what God has done for us in Jesus Christ, which all of us continually need.

I was struck years ago when a young woman, a daughter of ministry leaders, sought me out about her own sexual sin and after a few minutes said to me, "But, Ellen, children of Christian parents aren't supposed to struggle with these things!" My heart broke, and, honestly, I was frustrated as well. I think it was righteous frustration—how had she come to that conclusion, and who had taught her that Christians are beyond sexual temptation? Beyond sexual sin? Hebrews 4:16 beautifully reminds us that we are welcome at King Jesus's throne because we are his! There is no sign on the door to the throne room that says, "All needy sinners welcome except sexual sinners."

Jesus's earthly ministry was bold not only because he put himself in the presence of those whom society marginalized but also because he extravagantly poured his love out upon them. The woman at the well in John 4 was a bent-over, sexually broken woman. Jesus pursued and honored her and then challenged her to live a different way. The woman caught in the act of adultery in John 8 was a brokenhearted, bent-over woman. We don't know her reasons for giving way to sexual sin, but we know this: how humiliated she must have felt standing before a crowd of self-righteous onlookers; how terrified she must have been as she groveled on the ground, waiting for rocks to be hurled with brutal hatred so as to end her life. Jesus was there too: loving, speaking, forgiving, and calling her to new life.

2) Being Present with Sexual Strugglers

We follow in the footsteps of Jesus by intentionally being present with women who are sexual strugglers. We bring his presence to them and call their attention to his presence. But how do we find them? How do we draw near to them when they remain so hidden, so afraid to come forward for help? I serve with a ministry known to provide help for sexual strugglers, so in one sense it's easy for me. But inside or outside my office, I am seeking to grow in being present with women through sharing my own daily struggles and neediness for Jesus and his life-giving Word. I've learned that when I allow others to know aspects of my own bentness and how I'm seeking to walk by faith before God, walls slowly come down in the hearts of struggling women. When hurting women grasp that Jesus is not distant from us but, rather, present with us in our struggles and actually speaking to us by his Spirit through his Word, they discover his grace that woos us all to follow him.

This chapter on ministry to women in the midst of struggles with sexuality is meant to be read, of course, in light of the content of the other chapters of this book devoted to ministry among women. Ministry of the Word at the heart of it all, Titus 2 relationships among women in local churches and communities, along with understanding how God equips us to serve, will all be key ingredients as we seek also to be intentional disciplers of women who are sexual strugglers.[5]

3) Teaching the Word Fully and Compassionately

Ministering to sexually broken women, as they become known to us, must involve ongoing and specific teaching from the Word. Jesus was there to teach people in the synagogue that day, and we all need help learning, don't we? In our first conversation, Lauren told me that the few times her pastor or women's ministry leaders mentioned even the idea of sexual sin, they did so in only a general way. There was little specific context given, and the tone of the subject was distressingly judgmental: *Don't do this! It's wrong!* She'd heard teaching on the fact that sexual impurity is sin and generally why Christians should not be participating in it but zero teaching or discipleship on how to overcome it.

Women like Lauren and Tia need teachers, trusted sisters in Christ who will know them and then disciple them to understand the nature of temptation and what's happening in their hearts that is contributing to their sin. They also need help to understand the richness of God's good design for sexuality and not merely lists of do's and don'ts. Many dear Christian sisters who are caught up in sexual sin are longing to know if the Bible really has truth that will connect with them at the street level of emotional lust, sexual desires, and out-of-control thought lives. Certainly a faithful study of the Scriptures from beginning to end offers a comprehensive story of God's creation of sexuality as good, the perversion of sexuality as both literally sinful and consistently symbolizing rebellion against a God who loves us like a husband, and the consummation of God's redemptive plan pictured in terms of a grand wedding feast. Delving into Scripture's teaching uncovers not just truths about sexuality but, in the process, truths about the Lord God himself—personal truths that draw us toward him and away from sin.

But we can't just expect women to come running to be taught. Ministry to sexually broken women involves looking for ones who are hiding. I love the fact that this story tells us Jesus *saw* this woman, even as she was most likely at the back of the room, at best, and *called her* to himself (Luke 13:12). Women in the church are typically ignored when it comes to issues of sexual struggle. They are not called toward Christ because there is a lack of robust and compassionate biblical teaching that *names* sexual struggles as a women's issue too. Lust is seen primarily as a men's issue—as if women don't have a libido. When pastors and Christian leaders acknowledge that women are as human and as broken as men in the area of sexuality, then leadership in the church will address these areas as an aspect of our fallen humanity for which we all need the gospel. Like the woman who went to her pastor as a nineteen-year-old, many have had encounters with Christian leaders who really didn't want (or maybe didn't feel equipped) to speak gospel truth into areas of sexual sin.

In Luke 13 Jesus displays his extraordinary love and compassion. He moves gently toward the disabled woman, whose bentness is on display for everyone to see. He notices her, calls her to himself, and patiently waits for her to reach him. We can only wonder what she thought the crowd of men between her and Jesus might say or do. We don't know if there were other women sitting next to her who may have smiled and encouraged her to go to this teacher, Jesus, because he was known to welcome hurting people in his presence. But we know this: she responded to his call and came into his presence as a needy woman. And Jesus welcomed her. No longer hidden, no longer living on the margins of society, she came to the one who named her as an honored daughter of Abraham and who touched her broken body and healed her.

When women come to see me at my office, the fact that they are actually there speaks volumes to me. It's frightening to speak to someone and share your deepest secrets and feelings of shame. The courage and humility of women over the years in this regard has spurred me on in my walk of faith. I truly believe that when we ask God to help us to see people as he does, we grow in knowing how to receive them in a way that helps them feel safe to come and open up.

We need to ask ourselves, and others in our lives: How do I come across to others? Do I seem to have it all together? Do women feel safe to share the "fine china"[6] of their souls with me? Being a safe person doesn't mean we need to air all our secrets or use public teaching opportunities as a confessional for personal sin. It does mean, however, several things:

- Being willing to model repentance. Sharing our personal experiences of 1 Thessalonians 1:9–10 (being women who daily need help to turn to Jesus Christ from the idols that entice our hearts) is one of the ways we live out Titus 2 and "teach what is good."

- Growing as a wise and loving listener.

- Growing as a woman who uses her theology in a very practical, life-on-life way so that God's Word is applied to the real-life situations of women in our lives. Our discipling will then increasingly and fearlessly step into the messes of women's lives, helping them to see the temptations and patterns of sexual sin that they are blind to.

4) Being the Healing Hands of Jesus

How amazing that God uses us to bring the healing of Jesus into the lives of broken women and to share the joy of that healing among

God's people. He could just do it all himself. Jesus could have accomplished the healing in Luke 13 very privately. He could have noticed the woman and healed her simply with a loving thought as she sat in the back of the room. But Jesus makes her need for him and his love for her very public. He is showing and sharing his work. He proclaims words of freedom and healing over her and then, with holy God-hands, touches her. Imagine what this woman felt as she heard these miraculous words and then felt his tender, healing touch on her broken body. Imagine the wonder of the people witnessing this miracle as they "rejoiced at all the glorious things that were done by him" (v. 17). Jesus is near to the brokenhearted and to the sin-captive women in our lives, and he sends *us* to speak his love, to touch with his compassion, and to multiply rejoicing in his work.

We serve as instruments in the hands of God and ambassadors of healing grace as we bring his Word to women, applying gospel truths to sexual brokenness. "Then they cried to the LORD in their trouble, and he delivered them from their distress. He sent out his word and healed them, and delivered them from their destruction" (Ps. 107:19–20). To be intentional gospel ambassadors and Titus 2 women, in relation to sexual wholeness, will mean incorporating multiple levels of teaching and hands-on discipleship into our one-to-one mentoring relationships, our women's ministry small groups, our weekly women's Bible study ministry, and even our churches' women's retreats. We will aim to:

1. Offer clear biblical teaching about God's good design for sexuality.

2. Help women understand that the fall has impacted every detail of who we are.

3. Assure women that sexual temptation is a "common to all" trial that we will continue to face while we live on this earth and for which we need to be equipped, especially in these days when

sexual battles are pervasive and public. The equipping entails embracing our present Savior and through his Spirit learning how to flee idols, how to make no provision for the desires of the flesh, and how, practically, to "put on the Lord Jesus Christ" (see Rom. 13:8–14; 1 Cor. 10:13–14).

4. Exhort all women to commit to a lifestyle that is "in the light," which means *no hiding*. The beauty of Proverbs 28:13 is that along with the sober warning about hiding one's sins, there is a promise: "Whoever . . . confesses and forsakes them [his sins] will obtain mercy." God's Word commands us to walk in the light with one another (1 John 1:5–10), but all too often our discipleship ministries never seem to go very deep with people. This is because we stubbornly resist being real with one another, confessing our sins and helping one another forsake them. Freedom and flourishing, not only for sexually struggling women but for all of us in all our struggles, will happen only as we confess our real selves to God and to one another, pray for each other, and help one another apply grace and truth to all our struggles.

5. Incorporate all of the above into our ministry through illustrations, examples, and applications of passages we are studying. This does *not* mean that we need to talk about sex and sexuality every week. But to avoid it completely and never apply God's grace to this essential part of our humanity is to ignore a temptation that is common to all and that is much talked about in Scripture. This avoidance leads many struggling women to feel utterly alone and unsure about how God's Word applies to this area of life.

Tia amazed me when she brought in her Bible verse journal, a spiral-bound notebook packed with Scriptures that she was seeking to meditate on throughout the day. This mother of two toddlers knew that to take her thoughts captive, she needed to be diligent to fill her mind with God's Word and to pray the truths she was memorizing. She also committed to share the full extent of her struggles with two women in her community group whom I helped her identify as being safe to share with.[7] She also began to open up more in the marriage counseling sessions she and her husband had with their pastor and a lay counselor from their church. They were seeking help regarding their sexual intimacy problems, as well as the ongoing impact of her sexual abuse. In her conversations with me, Tia began to understand how same-sex desires had been cultivated in her life and how she could grow in loving and being increasingly sexually oriented to the one God had given to her: her husband. The battle was engaged by God's Word and among God's people.

Lauren admitted her habit of quickly jumping on her computer to look at porn whenever her roommates were out. So she made a commitment to go online only when her roommates were home and when she was in a common area of the house they shared. In addition, she committed to have accountability software put on her laptop, smartphone, and tablet.[8] She also took the brave but needed step of sharing with two classmates her temptations with pornography and solo-sex. To her surprise, she discovered that one of them had the exact same struggle. The other admitted a pattern of emotional dependence with her female friends and occasional fantasies about women. This second friend had recently asked her mentor for help, and, as it turned out, this older woman agreed to begin meeting with all three women. They began to meet for prayer, Bible study, and accountability as they shared a common desire to be godly single women who were increasingly taking steps of obedience in their paths of repentance and devotion to their Savior.

Being the healing hands of Jesus means pursuing the sexually broken and celebrating God's work in their lives—in spite of opposition. As the bent-over woman in Luke 13 experienced a miraculous healing, the religious leaders in the synagogue scoffed. The very ones who should have shown love and compassion to her did not care about her pain. They were passionately committed to the law and to things being done "right" in their religious community. Jesus's radical display of compassion sent him into a heated conflict with these men, and yet his response was to defend and celebrate this woman. He had no fear of the scorn and rebuke of the religious leaders who didn't like his disruption of the normal pattern of Sabbath-day activity. Our loving Lord was always working, even in the face of adversaries, to bring redemption and the good news of forgiveness, grace, healing, and new beginnings to the broken-bodied and brokenhearted.

How can we grow in recognizing and discipling women struggling with sexual sin and, like Jesus, not be swayed by opposition as we enter into broken lives? Perhaps the most fundamental question is whether we rejoice over the good news of the gospel, acknowledging that it does address all our brokenness, including the sexual brokenness of women, giving hope to those bent by their sexual sin. Many, many daughters of the Lord are longing for bold biblical teaching and gentle discipleship to guide them in repentance.

There may be those who, like the synagogue leaders, will oppose you, saying things such as: "Christian women don't struggle with those things! And even if they did, we shouldn't talk about such things at our women's ministry gatherings."

In 2013 when our women's discipleship curriculum, *Sexual Sanity for Women: Healing from Relational and Sexual Brokenness,* was published, I received an e-mail from a woman. She wrote: "You do know, right, that 99 percent of women in the church will never engage this? Most churches won't even consider this!" I was disheartened and initially angry. This workbook involved me in a long and difficult process. Didn't she appreciate the fact that we were willing to help churches address this topic?

After a day or two of prayer and reflection on her words, the

Holy Spirit comforted and challenged me. What if the woman was right? God seemed to be asking me: *Ellen, are the 1 percent worth it?* Somehow this question melted my anger and frustration because, without hesitation, my answer was yes. My heart was moved, remembering the faces of so many women who have engaged their sexual sin struggles with courageous repentance—women like Lauren and Tia who, like the bent-over woman, responded to the Lord's call to draw near to him in shame-filled, sensitive areas of struggle. Like the woman in Luke 13, they left their place of hiding and lonely struggle. With the help of godly people, they are growing in Christlikeness with an increasing pursuit of obedience and a decreasing pursuit of sin.

Perhaps some of you reading this chapter have encountered your own hidden areas of bentness and have experienced the compassionate presence of Jesus through his Word and his people. If so, you are marvelously prepared to be the healing hands of Jesus to others. He sends each one of us his forgiven children to sow his Word generously, extravagantly—sharing the gracious truths of grace, forgiveness, and rescue for all sinners, including sexual sinners. We cannot hoard the treasures of the gospel, applying them only to the areas of struggle with which we feel comfortable. Jesus sends us as his servants where and how he pleases, and this may mean going into places in the lives and hearts of women that we'd prefer not to know about. Maybe this means being a Titus 2 woman to someone bound up in sexual sin.

But should not these women, beloved daughters of God, be set free from the brokenness of sin and shame?

Yes, they should. The beloved of the Lord have not been created for bent-over lives but to be those who, having encountered Jesus, stand up in praise to our God. May King Jesus give us courage, wisdom, and joy in our ministry of seeing, calling, welcoming, discipling, and loving his precious daughters.

Gifts and Giftedness

Finding the Place to Serve

Kathleen Nielson and Gloria Furman

Women in complementarian contexts often discuss the question of whether there is a place for their gifts in the church. This chapter aims to offer an overwhelming and overwhelmingly encouraging *yes!* in answer to that question—along with a call for both men and women to cultivate and support the gifts of women more fully and fruitfully within their local congregations.

Gloria and I (Kathleen) worked on this chapter together, first distributing a simple questionnaire to eighteen women in various positions of ministry within strong, biblically based congregations where only men serve as elders and preach in the worship services. Ours is no scientific survey, but we are happy that the eleven actual respondents represent six different denominations (including independent churches), diverse regions of the United States, and six different countries.[1] They are Bible study leaders, directors of women's ministries, and pastors' wives involved in ministering to women. We have sought to gather from these women (and from many others more informally, in the course of our own travels and ministries) a glimpse of how women are serving in the church and how the church might encourage women to serve more and more fruitfully. Some women gave us permission to quote them—and we will. We are grateful to all the women who have shared with us their thoughts on this important topic.

The topic of how women use their gifts in the church warrants more space than a chapter allows. We aim to offer an encouraging glimpse—first, as I ask the question, *How is ministry among women happening now?* And then as Gloria asks the question, *How can the church encourage increasingly fruitful ministry among women?*

HOW IS MINISTRY AMONG WOMEN HAPPENING NOW?

Answer 1: Just Like It Happens Anywhere

Many women make this point first—and it certainly should come first. Women are first and foremost human beings created in the image of God and created together with men to be fruitful and multiply and fill the earth and subdue it and have dominion over it. Genesis 1 comes first. Every human being is created to hear and obey God's Word, and so, indeed, women and men and boys and girls must all be learning and living the Scriptures together. Among all his people God generously distributes gifts and abilities, wisdom and knowledge, and intelligence and skill, all for his glory and for the good of the body of Christ.

A good part of what women report women to be doing is simply what Christians in general should be doing: studying and sharing the Bible with others, music ministry, evangelism, nursery duty, discipling others, helping the elderly or disabled, praying with others, visiting the sick, working with finances or administration, designing or collating bulletins, preparing or serving meals. None of us can do all of these things all of the time, but all believers share the call to share our gifts with the other sheep in the flock and the sheep who are being called to join the flock.

The fact that the authoritative teaching/ruling role of elders is to be filled by qualified men (1 Tim. 2:12; 5:17) puts a guard around that particular channel of service *and* opens wide the other channels through which men and women alike are called to use their gifts to serve. There are dangers in all directions, of course: not only that we might lose Scripture's clear teaching but also that in the process of keeping it we might add to it, or that the important biblical restrictions on one channel would somehow minimize the value of the other channels. Most women I meet have personally encountered these dangers in one form or another, as have I.

What we want to highlight here, however, are the stories that don't get told often enough: the stories of good and fruitful ministry among women. These stories are all around us; perhaps they sometimes don't get told simply because the people in them are busy getting on with it. Most of the respondents to our questionnaire claim not a perfect balance of tensions within their congregations but a healthy involvement of women in multiple channels of service. You would visit many of their church gatherings and see both women and men greeting, perhaps, or ushering or singing or reading Scripture or giving testimonies or listed in the worship folders as heading up various ministries or committees. Fully engaged complementarian ministry is not only possible; it is happening on many fronts, and it is beautiful when the parts work together. It is heartbreaking when they don't. There is much room for growth, as we shall discuss. But there is much vibrant life to report.

How is ministry among women happening now? First, *just like it happens anywhere*. Women and men are in this together, as human beings created by God and called to follow him according to his Word.

But here's the pointed question: If men and women are distinct as male and female from the beginning, then what difference does this distinction make in the life of the church? If Scripture gives men and women not identical but complementary roles, as we have discussed (see especially chapter 2), both in marriage and in the church, then what difference do these roles make in ministry in general? These distinctions must have ramifications.

Answer 2: With Distinct Teaching and Discipling Roles

Although ministry among women happens in large part just like it happens anywhere, it is crucial to recognize its distinctions, particularly in a complementarian context. If we believed that women's and men's roles are indistinguishable, then we might expect their ministries to be largely indistinguishable, and there would be little impetus to develop women's ministries. However, if we believe that women's and men's roles are distinctive, then we might expect their ministries to have some distinctions as well. The basic fact that the elder role is to be filled by only qualified men means that all women in a complementarian church are called to pursue ministry under the authoritative leadership of persons of the opposite gender—this is distinctive. It requires Spirit-filled stretching from both sides.

The most concrete outcome of these distinct roles is the one Paul clarifies in 1 Timothy 2:12, and it's not hard to see why this point needs clarifying. As people meant to live on God's Word, we will constantly be teaching it to one another, and women are clearly often just as good teachers as men (sometimes better). Consider Priscilla, for example. And yet women are not to be in a position of authoritatively teaching men, because of something inherent in the very order of creation, as 1 Timothy 2 goes on to explain (see chapter 2). The concrete outcome here is not just that women don't preach to men but also that women must find the proper context in which to preach or teach.[2] That context often turns out to be one in which women come together to study the Bible, teach one another, and thereby model for one another what godly, articulate womanhood looks like; it looks like being Word-filled women, women who clearly understand and pass on the Scriptures through both life and teaching.

The woman-to-woman teaching that Paul commends to Titus has its good, practical side, but it comes in a book whose whole point is that godly behavior flows out of gospel truth; they must go together. (See chapter 7 for further discussion of Titus 2.) If we women are teaching each other just practical tips or even just the Bible's teaching on womanhood, then we're missing the deep truths out of which those life lessons flow; we must teach the whole Bible as the foundation of it all. Most of the responders to our questionnaire (and many women in our experience) are full of enthusiasm for Bible study among women in their churches—not to replace other interaction with the body of Christ, including regular worship gatherings and small groups and whatever means of growth church leadership fosters but, rather, to encourage women to become (and help each other become) active receivers and sharers of God's Word.

Bible study among women happens in all kinds of ways. At College Church in Wheaton, for example, hundreds of women gather weekly to study books of the Bible together, to meet in small groups to discuss the work they've done at home, and then to hear a plenary exposition given by one of the women teachers. I was part of that study for many years and witnessed the Word changing lives, as women shared it with one another and shared their lives in the process. But in many contexts today Bible study is happening less formally and more organically: women are reading and teaching the Bible to each other one-to-one (reports Leonie Mason, from St. Helens Bishopsgate in London); "one spiritually mature woman has discipled and encouraged countless women over the years" (Linda Green, The Orchard Evangelical Free Church, Arlington Heights, IL); and "women are actively involved in evangelism and discipling other women°. . . by visiting homes of friends and praying for one another and reading Scripture together . . . and in a Bible study in which the older women teach the younger women of the church" (Hepzibah Shekhar, Zion Church, Uttar Pradesh, India).

Answer 3: In the Form of Women Helping Women

The ministry of the Word connects to other kinds of distinctive ministry among women. Because God established from the beginning that women are the ones to become wives and mothers, women— even those who do not marry or have children—share experiences that set them apart. How is ministry among women happening? It is happening as women reach out to help one another with the safety and understanding that the presence of another woman brings.

It was remarkable to observe the patterns of women helping women in the respondents' comments. That woman from Linda Green's church who discipled countless others now has some impaired hearing and so cares for the children of younger women who are being trained in discipleship. Not all but much of the help relates to women helping other women with child-related issues. In many low-income areas of the United States and the world, women are struggling together to raise their children, with few men and very few godly men present in their lives. Patricia Henry (Metropolitan Evangelistic Church, Cape Town, South Africa) reports that many churches are made up of more than 80 percent women, largely due to adverse effects of the South African apartheid system. "Family units in the community are comprised mostly of women leading single-parent families with a visible absence of fathers." Therefore, the church truly becomes family for these women, who value the leadership of the male elders and who help one another in remark-

able ways: "The women's fellowship is by far the largest ministry
. . . and provides a forum for mutual encouragement, accountability, and outreach to other women suffering through similar trials."

The following is just one of Patricia's many vivid descriptions of
a woman she compares to the biblical Dorcas (we'll call her "Dorcas" to protect her identity):

> "Dorcas" is a widow (lost her husband to gang violence three
> years ago) who came to faith while imprisoned for being a drug
> mule and has been walking faithfully with the Lord for seven
> years now. She has two daughters and a son—only the eldest
> daughter is walking with Christ. In the block of flats where she
> stays, where she had been feared before, she now commands a
> great deal of respect from the community, because the evidence
> of her changed life in Christ is clearly visible. She feeds over
> forty children at her small home twice a week with a hot meal
> and supports this feeding scheme by "hawking," i.e., she sells
> household detergents that she bottles herself, and walks through
> the community during all her free time, pushing her supermar-
> ket trolley with her goods. She also cares for many sick and
> elderly folks in the community (with house and hospital visits),
> and sees her social responsibility and opportunity to share the
> gospel with them as a natural outflow of her gratitude to God
> for her salvation. The church has not been able to financially
> support what she does, but she sees what she is doing as an
> integral part of her life within the church family.

"Dorcas" is helping the women around her for the sake of the
gospel. This is a glimpse of women's ministry we all need to see.

Interestingly, "Dorcas" is also the name of a women's ministry
reported by Esther Lopez de Ramirez from the Evangelical Presbyterian Church of Peru, Los Rosales, Cajamarca, Peru. Women
in this ministry administrate the significant resources channeled
through missionary support and organize sales and distribution,

thereby overseeing a large population of children in the community, who are clothed and cared for—and taught the Bible and the Westminster Shorter Catechism.

I'll never forget teaching a women's Bible study group in the Kibera slum of Nairobi, Kenya. It was a group largely comprised of HIV-positive women who seemingly would have sat there for hours on end listening to the Word taught through a translator—with babies squirming in arms and crawling all over the dirt floor. What I remember, besides their rapt attention to the teaching, are the stories of how those women would take one another's children when one of them came to die. Even though they lived in the poorest circumstances, there they were, in a Bible study of Kibera Reformed Presbyterian Church, learning the Word and helping each other (and each other's children) survive day by day. That was ministry among women.

All kinds of women have ministry needs that other women can often best meet. Christine Hoover from Charlottesville Community Church in Virginia tells of several groups they have targeted, including "a large number of college students, many of whom have questions about sexuality and dealing with past or current sexual sin. We have women who have come out of sexual sin who are eager and willing to counsel young women about purity and making godly dating decisions." Certainly in relation to a whole range of sexual issues it is helpful for women to deal with women. Or in relation to shared contexts: there in Virginia, one medical resident's wife has "used her experience to reach out to the large population of residents' wives in our city." Their church has a women's ministry team comprised of six women who oversee not only Bible study but these other aspects of ministry as well.

We're not talking about help separate from sharing God's Word. Sandra Smith (New City Fellowship, Chattanooga, Tennessee) describes the helpful relationships that have grown out of a women's Sunday school class taught by an African-American woman and a white woman together: "This class draws women from cross-cultural and cross-generational backgrounds and multiple economic and educational levels. Women are connecting across these barriers to take hold of and celebrate the gospel of Jesus. Informal mentoring is taking place and young and old are learning from each other."

Hepzibah Shekhar puts it well: "Often women in distress or in need will seek support of other women, and God often uses such situations to bring these women and their families to him, when Christian women rally around them and pray for them and share the gospel with them." Teach us, Indian women.

Answer 4: In Relation to Male Leadership

We pointed out one distinctive of ministry among complementarian women: they believe in pursuing ministry under the authoritative leadership of persons of the opposite gender. We also mentioned the "stretch" required from both sides—as women learn to "learn quietly with all submissiveness" (1 Tim. 2:11), and elders learn to lead with loving, unselfish wisdom. Of course, it is significant that lay men as well must learn to submit to elder leadership. But their submission is somewhat different, being *without* the specific command not to teach or to exercise authority over the opposite gender, and *with* the possibility of themselves becoming elders should they be found qualified. In the complementarian context, it is impossible to talk about ministry among women apart from talking about women's unique relationship with the elders who are leading them. Women's ministry happens in relation to male leadership.

We don't just all do certain things within the church body; rather, we live in ordered and variously crisscrossed relationships with one another—parents and children, husbands and wives, elders and lay people, men and women. This is the ecclesial landscape. It is a beautiful landscape, designed by God for our joy and for his glory. We can surely mess it up from all sides, and we often do. But our messes do not change the inherent goodness of God's ordained order.

I visit a lot of churches and women's events, in the process observing many dynamics of ministry among women. What I have found is that with the most supportive relationships between women and male elders (usually pastors, so I will use that title) comes some of the most joyful and fruitful ministry among women. If the women are just sort of independently carrying on their separate ministries, they can lack direction from the church and connection with the church. In the end they will be less supportive and fruitful in the growth of the whole church.

But when there's clearly encouraging support in both directions, women and men spur each other on in all sorts of ways. Occasionally a pastor sends me a note in advance of an event, saying he's praying for God's blessing as I prepare; that means a lot and reveals a lot. Sometimes a pastor is there to greet and bless and pray for the women as an event begins, and the women are indeed blessed and responsive. Sometimes a meal or meeting is arranged with women in various positions of leadership, along with a pastor or pastors, and we all discuss together issues related to Bible study methods and materials and training, some of which might pertain to both men and women and some to women only.

Many fruitful ministry interconnections quickly become apparent in such mutually supportive relationships, as men and women together are praying for and sharing insights into various families, planning harmonizing ministry strategies, etc. At our women's conferences of The Gospel Coalition, it means the world to the thousands of women attending not just to have excellent women teachers but also to have TGC leaders, those several men who come and care and join so heartily in the teaching. Such supported ministry among women draws them in to the church, helping them in turn to support the various levels of leadership around them—all of which ultimately helps build up the whole church.

Questionnaire respondents joined many voices in both Gloria's and my experience expressing appreciation for pastoral support *and* the need for more support: spiritual and theological and material (as in financial). Kathy Keller of Redeemer Presbyterian Church in New York City puts this need quite straightforwardly; she is one of many talking about the important priority of hiring female staff members: "Pastors who believe that women are equally made in the image of God to rule creation need to make that apparent by their practices." Christine Hoover comments that women "serve fruitfully when they know that they are a valued part of the church and when their ministries are highlighted and God's work in them is celebrated."

In a visit to Sydney, Australia, I shared a lovely tea with a group of strong, godly women who serve in mostly paid ministry positions throughout that city—all strong complementarians, ministering in male-led churches and all not only trained theologically but also in the process of training other women—many of whom were in official church internship positions. I looked around and asked, "How did this happen?" Their response was first (not only, but first) to credit the strong leadership of men who (like the apostle Paul) valued women as crucially important coworkers in the gospel (see Phil. 4:3). That part of the landscape in Sydney was beautiful indeed.

Visiting a strong Reformed seminary in the United States, I again shared tea, this time with a roomful of women students. In a Q&A time, their urgent question to me was, "Is there a place in the church for us to serve?" I looked at this group of godly, eager, theologically trained women and with all my heart said a loud yes! There is a place for women to serve. It will not always be the perfect place we envision. We might be called to do things we didn't plan or want to do along the way. Dorcas doesn't always get paid what she deserves. But we must indeed serve—with quiet, submissive, prayerful, relentless strength—because we are serving our Lord. We are serving the church he loves, for whom he died.

And, as we serve, we must call the leadership of the church (or, perhaps more important, the leadership must call the church) to make more and more places for women to serve, to encourage training for those places, and to support service in those places both with celebration and with finances. Along the way, we must serve humbly, "learn[ing] quietly with all submissiveness" (1 Tim. 2:11), respecting and praying for the elders of our churches and always looking for fruitful opportunities for dialogue and growth. (See also chapter 4's discussion of the context of church leadership.) Listen to what Hepzibah Shekhar reports happened to "Sister S," from Zion Church in Uttar Pradesh:

> "Sister S" (name withheld for security purposes) is a godly woman and a praying woman. She is bold in evangelism and has always been very active in sharing the gospel. . . . She was from a poor family, and therefore she would go to different people's homes and do the dishes and cleaning to earn some extra money and support her family. In the midst of all this she continued to be faithful and prayed for [her unbelieving husband], fulfilled her responsibilities at home, and yet reached out to other women and shared the gospel with them. Eventually the Lord was kind to change her husband's heart, and the church saw her love for the Lord and evangelism and took her on as a woman's worker and an evangelist in order to free her and give her more time to reach out to other women in similar difficult situations. She has shared the gospel with hundreds of women, prayed with hundreds of them, and seen dozens of women come to the Lord and several families changed.

Answer 5: With Variations according to Context—but with One Central Theme

How is ministry among women happening now? It's happening *just like it happens anywhere*. It's happening *with distinct teaching and discipling roles*. It's happening *in the form of women helping women*. It's happening *in relation to male leadership*. And, finally, it's happening *with variations according to context—but with one central theme*.

No one formula perfectly encourages women to use their gifts in ministry. Churches work differently according to different denominations and cities and cultures. Some urban churches are filled with single, professional women and men who serve in all kinds of ways, and in that context some of the more distinctive woman-to-woman helping ministries may be less emphasized, although they are surely there. Many small churches simply don't have much funding to develop programs and staff, although the church of "Sister S" certainly stands out! Churches in economically struggling areas are often filled mostly with women helping each other survive—and often ministering powerfully in the process. Some churches have thriving programs that teach women the Bible and encourage them in ministry, and many of those churches are growing a vision to train up more women teachers and leaders to carry it on.

Ministry among women happens variously according to context—but with one central theme: at the heart of these diverse glimpses of ministry is a passion for the gospel. What comes through is a desire not so much to use gifts but to see the church grow as people come to know Jesus Christ and follow his Word. If that gospel motivation is not in our hearts, then service is useless and gifts are vain. Linda Green senses the need for a renewed focus on the gospel among women; for many who don't fit in to church activities, it's not always that there's not a place for them. Too often it's that "rather than examining their hearts and realigning their priorities through the lens of the gospel, they are investing their lives in the things of this world, failing to understand the eternal significance of the church and that it is worth their best efforts and time." What we're after, Linda writes, "has to start, continue, and be fueled in every way by the gospel for the glory of Christ."

HOW CAN THE CHURCH ENCOURAGE INCREASINGLY FRUITFUL MINISTRY AMONG WOMEN? (GLORIA)

We've seen evidence from this small sampling of women serving in local churches across the globe that women who are in Christ have been given divine enablements for ministry. We have grown a greater appreciation for the fact that each member of the body of Christ has a particular function designed and enabled by God—including women. So, how could the church *better* envision and encourage ministry among such gifted women?

As Christians we understand that men and women are first and foremost human beings created in God's image. God created us to be his thoughtful image bearers and to live hearing and responding rightly to his Word. With such a starting point, Christians cannot share many of the world's views of women: we must deny that women derive their importance or significance from their body parts, relationships, fertility, marital status, skills, or employment. The world cannot give us the foundation and direction we need. We look to our creator God and to his Word to govern us as we seek to cast vision and encourage ministry among women.

Considering the aim of Paul's and Peter's instructions to the early churches, no doubt their words regarding stewardship of gifts were directed toward both women and men. Women have been strategic in the building up of the body of Christ since the very birth of the church in Acts. As the apostles preached and pastored, women were among those who were converted, began serving as colaborers, and went on cross-cultural missions. The examples of many such women are all over the New Testament. Paul, who often bears the brunt of misunderstanding regarding the role of women in the family and church, actually engaged in radically counter-cultural practices in treating women as colaborers in the gospel. For example, at the end of his epistle to the Romans Paul sends his greetings to twenty-eight people by name, and one-third are women. Any apprehension we have about relying on the Bible to give us a vision for investing in women ought to be put to rest. For more reasons than one, we may have utter confidence in the Bible as a trustworthy guide for steering our conversations about how to better encourage women in their gifts. With the Bible to direct us, we might arrive at the following seven action points.

Contextualize the Bridges for Service Opportunities

Like the apostle Peter, we believers value women as coheirs of the grace of life (1 Pet. 3:7). We, therefore, repudiate every demonic lie that says women are "less than." Church leaders and lay people alike need to champion gladly the biblical worldview that every human being is created to hear and obey God's Word and therefore enthusiastically to remove obstacles and build bridges so that every woman can hear and obey God's Word—from Genesis to Revelation. The obstacles may present themselves differently all over the world. Consider the example of Hepzibah Shekhar and the Indian women who experience trouble leaving their homes at night:

> One of the biggest challenges in women's ministry in our context is that most women are not very independent, they don't have their own transport, and they cannot drive, and it's often not safe being out alone in the evenings. Any ministry that is done has to keep these things in mind. So for every activity that women undertake, it often means that we have to find volunteers who can drive them and chaperone them, and we also have to find babysitters—but most importantly everything has

to be finished before dark. (Hepzibah Shekhar, Zion Church, Lucknow, Uttar Pradesh, India)

A mix of practical hindrances besets us. Pam Brown, of Trinity Bible Church in South Sutton, New Hampshire, comments on busyness as an obstacle: "Most wives and moms are overwhelmed with the juggling act of family, work, and church." Leeann Stiles of Redeemer Church in Dubai names a few more practical issues:

> Our church is four years old and has grown rapidly. We have an amazing demographic: over fifty nationalities and people from all walks of life. . . . However the rapid and diverse growth is not without challenges particularly in drawing people into fellowship with each other. New people sometimes slip through the cracks. We meet in a hotel, so mid-week gatherings are scattered around the city. Many members work six days a week.

Our bridges for equipping women to serve in ministry must be contextualized. Compare the iron and steel Golden Gate Bridge in San Francisco to the living root bridges made from trees that span the mighty rivers in Cherrapunji, India. These conduits, constructed on opposite sides of the planet, are worlds apart visually but the same functionally. The bridges we need to build in our local churches will look different depending on the context, but their function will serve to build up women and equip them for fruitful service unto the Lord.

In India, women need dependable drivers and daylight ministry. From New Hampshire to Dubai, women need intentional, efficient, and personal means of connecting. In most contexts, child care is an issue. In some contexts women need help with reading or language skills. In many contexts, women need to learn of their need to read and study and share the Word—and their capacity to do so. All these bridges lead to the end of women growing together in the Word, and serving the body of Christ effectively in light of that Word.

As God's called-out image bearers who have been given the

mind of Christ and instructed to pray for God's readily available wisdom when we are lacking, we believers are never at a disadvantage when it comes to building bridges so that women can hear and obey God's Word. What are the obstacles in your local church that hinder women from the ministry of the Word? What hinders them from even more fruitful ministry? God's wisdom is sufficient for the bridge building that needs to take place in all of our ministry all over the world.

Teach about Stewardship

As they cross those bridges, how should women regard themselves, particularly in relation to their service and ministry in the church? God's Word tells us that all Christians, women included, need to be equipped with a stewardship mentality regarding their gifts. The term "gift" (*charisma*) (See Rom. 12:6; 1 Cor. 1:7; 12:4, 9, 28, 30–31; 1 Tim. 4:14; 2 Tim. 1:6) reveals that gifts are not all about us but mark us out as recipients of "God's varied grace."

This is especially critical to understand, because stewards are managers, not owners (cf. Luke 12:42; 16:1, 3, 8; 1 Cor. 4:1–2; Gal. 4:2; Titus 1:7). Sadly, our sinful inclination is toward self-seeking, and our hearts are capable of making spiritual gifts all about us. We like to see ourselves as proprietors, using our gifts for self-actualization and meeting our own needs. We feel happy when we are serving using our gifts, hearing feedback from people who have been blessed, and we can be duped into seeking this sense of self-satisfaction rather than being faithful to God. When we teach about gifts and facilitate service opportunities, we should be careful not to communicate (intentionally or otherwise) that spiritual gifts are a boost for our self-esteem, a means to establish our identity, or an indication of our worth.

The gifts have an outward focus, as they all (both speaking and serving gifts) have an aim to build up the body of Christ. If a woman has speaking gifts, she ought to endeavor to speak words that are in accordance with God's Word. If she has serving gifts, she ought to endeavor to serve in such a way that she is serving with the strength that God supplies. When women engage in ministry in this manner, then the gift, the strength, the fruit, and the glory are all to the praise of God's glory (1 Pet. 4:10–11). It behooves the church to teach and model a stewardship mentality: we are to develop and do good with our gifts because God is the one who has given them for strengthening others. Women who find themselves in service opportunities they did not envision for themselves, or women who hear themselves called to serve in places they do not personally enjoy, will be refreshed to remember that God has called them to faithfulness. And he will supply their every need. Truly, this kind of gift-stewarding is happening among women all over the world, as you read in some of the examples above.

Prioritize Theological Training

We need to aim for progress in building bridges and teaching stewardship and, in general, encouraging women to be biblically healthy and active members of a congregation. But why? To what end? We need to impress upon women (and men!) that church activity is not something that falls under the realm of extracurricular endeavors, something one might simply add to a CV or university application. Church activity, biblically speaking, is the body of Christ flexing its muscles—building itself up in love and reaching out to a lost world with the love of Christ. We don't send our children to mid-week youth activities merely to "keep them off the street and out of trouble." Neither do we women participate in ministry to "have something to occupy our time." Contra the misconception that women's ministry is simply a social venue, there is something profoundly theological and eschatologically oriented about ministry among women.

We must be rid, once and for all, of the gross misunderstanding that investing theological training in a woman will undermine her husband's authority, or diminish her femininity, or sour her gentle and quiet spirit. This misunderstanding belies an errant view of holiness and sanctification and assumes that the effect of sound doctrine and theological training is bloating people with loveless knowledge.

If we want to see the gospel continue to go forth through the ministry of women (as Paul and Peter did), then women need not only to be trained theologically but also to be trained in *the process of training other women* (see chapter 3). This will infuse a breath of fresh air into any one-to-one discipleship relationships that have forgotten the vision for multiplication. What might the Lord do through his daughters' service if every local church took up the costly (yet rewarding) work of training women in theology?

> The church can help women by providing theologically driven training and by not relegating the women to the corner under the "women's ministry" banner. (Christine Hoover, Charlottesville Community Church, Charlottesville, Virginia)

> At the moment, our greatest task is to keep this huge volunteer force motivated in gospel work, so our focus has been to provide adequate spiritual care and support for them. We believe that when they are spiritually well nurtured, the natural outflow of their lives will show more fruit in their service. (Patricia Henry, Metropolitan Evangelistic Church, Cape Town, South Africa)

> The church should organize training and service workshops in a specific community with urgent needs to meet and put what we learn in practice immediately. (Esther Lopez de Ramirez, Evangelical Presbyterian Church of Peru, Los Rosales, Cajamarca, Peru)

Appreciate the Varieties

What do any of us have that has not been given to us by God? Women, also, have received varieties of gifts from God (all manifestations of the grace of God) to be used in the building up of the body of Christ. There's a running joke with my friend Katie that she has the spiritual gift of pumpkin chocolate chip bread, because she is an outstanding baker and shares her gift at Bible studies and fellowship gatherings. But all jesting aside, since her talent and resources are God-given, and the exercise of her ministry is Spirit-filled, and her service is aimed to support the building up of the church, then we ought to give God the glory that is due to him in response to his abundant grace through Katie.

The church needs every woman in the body of Christ to be engaged in service, rooted and grounded in love, so that we can comprehend with all the saints what is the breadth and length and height and depth of the love of Christ (Eph. 3:17–18). In the fruitful use of our gifts we get to behold the various aspects of grace, which makes a healthy local church quite a sight to see. We have a corporate interest in seeing women fruitfully serving with the gifts they have been given. Being members of one another means that we have a vested interest in our fellow members' using their gifts productively. In order to experience all the geometrical dimensions of Christ's love, it's going to take the whole body of Christ, all the parts and joints, working. More fruitful ministry by women can happen when their varied gifts are recognized and their effects of edification validated.

Teach Women Church History

Biblically based validation of one another's gifts is especially important in a world that offers many other attractive, aggressive, and unbiblical systems of validation. The messages that women hear from the world are legion. Many of our survey respondents noted that women receive conflicting messages about their identity and purpose.

They suggested with confident hope that women would serve more fruitfully if they were taught about identity and purpose from a biblical worldview. After all, who but the church will engender in women a biblical perspective of themselves and the reason they are here?

There is one glaring, obvious application of this challenge: to consistently teach both men and women the scriptural understanding of identity in Christ and God's good design for his gendered image bearers. But there is one subtle application that we might miss: to celebrate the embodied application when we see it. There is a great cloud of witnesses surrounding us presently *and* urging us on from the past, and we do ourselves a disservice when we fasten our blinders on and miss their encouraging witness to us. Certainly the women mentioned in this chapter (and other chapters) serve as vibrant examples of sisters engaged in fruitful ministry among women. We might also look to church history and study the biographies of women of the past who smiled at the future because they held fast to the truth that their Redeemer lives.

The women in our churches need to be encouraged by the faithful ministry of women who have gone before us—Lucia, Blandina, Perpetua, Betty Stam, Betty Olsen, Ann Judson, Amy Carmichael, Lottie Moon, Sarah Edwards, and others. I have both seen and experienced the strengthening effect of considering the contributions of these predecessors in the faith. Women are better able to see their gifting in light of the big picture when they can step back and see what they have in common with these women of whom the world is not worthy. We are daughters of the same Father, are saved through faith in the same Savior, are gifted by the same Spirit, and are striving toward the same goal.

Leverage the "Women's Privilege"

A good number of these predecessors in the faith served as missionaries and understood the principle of leveraging the "women's privilege." Amy Carmichael was practicing this principle when she sat with various women hidden away in many back rooms of houses in the south of India. Mission agencies have practiced for years what churches in Eastern contexts do instinctively. When certain situations are presented as ministry opportunities, they send the women.

In many least-reached people groups there exist strict social rules in which the activities of women are closely monitored and restricted. Social interaction between nonrelative men and women is not only frowned upon in many of these cultures but forbidden. Many women spend their entire lives within the confines of their homes without access to school, travel, or nonrelative socializing. Women in these hard-to-reach societies do not need to be written off as those who could never have a chance to hear the good news, because women are privileged to be able to reach them. Even more fruitful ministry by women can happen when they understand their "women's privilege" in these contexts.

Even ministering in communities where women are marginalized, abused, raped, and murdered in the womb, the privilege of being a woman is obvious. Christian women are gifted by the Spirit to serve these women in ways that men cannot—through their affirming presence, nonthreatening physical touch, and gentle faith with a backbone of steel. May we never inadvertently describe God's good design for his daughters as a hindrance to the fruitful ministry to which he has called us.

Persistently Pray for Change

At one point in my (Gloria's) city's recent history it was reported that over one-half of the world's cranes were operating in this small strip of coastline on the Arabian Gulf. The city is under constant construction. It seems like overnight a sand dune can be inverted into a massive hole, which is then filled in with a concrete foundation for a new skyscraper. This kind of rapid change is possible in many churches, but in others the soil may not be so accepting. I'm thinking of a church elder I know who prayed for close to a decade that his church would not only embrace a biblical view of evangelism and missions through church planting but would also readily accept the challenges of sacrificial giving in order to make that happen. The Lord answered his prayers over the years through ordinary means. God equipped this church with elders who had a like-minded vision for the nations, financial capital through faithful giving, lay people discipling one another, and leaders ready to launch into the unknowns of church planting. I understand that some of you may feel deep frustration in your heart when it comes to the subject of your church's view of women in ministry. When change seems slow in coming, we must not flag in our faithful prayers that God would glorify himself in our midst. Radical change in church culture may come overnight, and it may come through steady plodding and ordinary means.

As we are patient in prayer, we need to approach awkward situations with grace. Holding fast to our commitment to Scripture as our authority, we must graciously acknowledge the ambiguity of so many situations that women find themselves in. For example, many missionary women have an afflicted conscience because of the ministry tasks they are presented with in their work, due to the lack of men on the mission field. Since the role of elder is restricted to men, it behooves our Christian brothers to aspire to the role of elder in cross-cultural contexts, and their sisters ought to encourage them in this. We have a need for discernment given to us by the Spirit of God, who will always lead us into holiness and decisions that will honor our Lord.

By the extraordinary grace of God, ordinary Christian women faithfully pursue their radical calling to follow Christ in everyday ways. We've seen in this chapter that *ordinary* is relative, and that no service done with the strength that God supplies is less than glorious. In summary, let us rejoice in God's wisdom in creating men and women differently and setting them apart for distinctive roles! As Linda Green so poignantly says,

> When women stop comparing themselves and competing with men in the home and church and begin to understand the powerful influence of a godly woman (along with recognizing their dependence on God's Word, prayer, and discipleship), they will begin to find great joy in complementing the men they serve alongside for the glory of the gospel. They will stop focusing on the couple of positions Scripture has designated for men and begin seeing the endless opportunities that are available for women to use whatever gifts God has given them. As they see how they can uniquely glorify Christ and his gospel in ways that men cannot, they begin to find great joy in doing what they may have seen as meaningless work before. (Linda Green, The Orchard Evangelical Free Church, Arlington Heights, Illinois)

May prayerful dependence on God be the posture of our heart as we consider how we might contextualize bridges for ministry among women, teach the biblical view of stewarding gifts, prioritize the theological training of women, appreciate the variety of ways the Spirit works through us, humbly reflect on the examples of women who have gone before us, and discern ways to leverage the "women's privilege" in service to our Lord. Expectant enthusiasm should mark our outlook. We've been given the Word of God to illumine our path and the Spirit to lead us. May the Lord be pleased as his daughters seek to serve in his name and for his glory.

PART 4

THE END OF
WOMEN'S
MINISTRY

— 10 —

Ultimate Goals

Heading for That Day

Nancy Guthrie

Doesn't it sometimes seem like we spend a lot of the days in our lives focused on some day in the future? When we were little, perhaps we counted down the days to our next birthday, full of anticipation. (Not so much anymore, right?) When we were in school we looked forward to that last day of school that would launch us into a season of fun and freedom. (Of course, on that same day parents probably started counting down to the day when school would start again.) Some of us have carefully planned a trip and have counted down the weeks and days until the day comes to set off on our adventure. Some have had a wedding date or a baby due date set out in the future, and we have counted down the days.

But I suppose there are also days set out before us that we

dread—the day the divorce is final, the day scheduled for the operation, the day we have to say good-bye.

There is a day spoken of throughout Scripture—a day of divine intervention in human history called "the day of the Lord," or sometimes simply "the day" or "that day." It is described as a day of burdens lifted (Isa. 10:27), thanksgiving, honor, relationship, grace, love, building, dancing, enjoyment, gladness, salvation, redemption, refreshment, rejoicing, joy, comfort, abundance, satisfaction, intimacy, forgiveness, and reward (Jer. 30:19–31:40); learning, peace, safety, and healing (Micah 4); cleansing and belonging (Zechariah 13). It sounds like a day to long for. And it is. But this is not all the Bible tells us about that day.

We also discover in the Scriptures that the day of the Lord will be a day of humiliation (Isa. 2:12); destruction (Isa. 13:2; Joel 1:15); cruelty (Isa. 13:9); doom (Ezek. 30:3); darkness (Amos 5:18); retribution (Obadiah 15); distress, anguish, ruin, and devastation (Zeph. 1:15); fire (Mal. 4:1); exposure (2 Pet. 3:10); and battle (Rev. 16:14). When we read these descriptions, this day does not exactly seem like something we should gladly anticipate but, rather, a day to dread.

So which is it? Will the day of the Lord—the day that Christ returns—be a day of mourning or a day of joy? Will it be a day of destruction or a day of restoration? Will it be a day of incredible loss or a day of indescribable gain?

The reality is that it will be both. For those who have feared the Lord by believing his gospel and are joined to Christ by faith, the day that is set out in the future by God, the day when he will intervene in human history, it is worth waking up every day wondering, with an eager heart, if this will be the day. But for those who have rejected God's offer of mercy and ignored God's gracious invitation into the safety of his fold, it is a day worth waking up every morning thinking about with a sense of sickening fear.

It is because this day is surely coming that ministry among women today really matters. In fact, ministry among women will matter forever because women are facing forever.

Perhaps we lose sight of that at times. It is easy for ministry among women to be mostly about the here and now—the realities that we can see with our eyes, the things we see as our most significant needs and challenges. We can tend to come to the Bible and take women to the Bible seeking to discover the answers to what we see as our most urgent questions but often looking primarily for comfort in temporal troubles. We can spend so much time focused on coping strategies and improvement plans for this life that we simply squeeze out both hopeful and sober consideration of the life to come—the forever that will begin on that day the Bible points us toward again and again—the day that will mark the beginning of forever joy and rest in the presence of God or forever misery away from his presence.

As we come to the conclusion of this book about ministry among women, let's consider the ultimate goal for such ministry. Clearly the ultimate goal of God's work in the world, the ultimate end of the history of God's redemptive purposes in the world, is what will have only begun on the day we read about as the culmination of human history—the day of the Lord—that day when finally the earth will be filled with the knowledge of the glory of the Lord as the waters cover the sea (Hab. 2:14). The greatest tragedy of life would be to face that day unprepared.

Perhaps this sets before us the highest aim of ministry among women: to prepare women for that great and terrible day. Surely if we prepare women to do good work in the world and to have good relationships and to be good wives and moms but don't prepare them for that day, then we have ultimately failed. Will not all of our sound theology and creative communications and interesting events and well-attended gatherings be in vain if our ministry among women does not result in being surrounded by the women God has placed in our lives now, when we stand before him on that day?

Sadly, many ministries that spend any time teaching about the day of the Lord tend to spend most of that time focused on trying to connect biblical prophecies to modern-day events and nations and people, as if what is most important about that day is knowing whether it will come about in our lifetime. Evidently this focus is nothing new. In Matthew 24 we read that in the week before Jesus was crucified, the disciples came to him privately, asking, "Tell us, when will these things be, and what will be the sign of your coming and of the end of the age?" (Matt. 24:3).

Jesus's primary response was that no one except his Father knows when this day will be. Rather than focus on the *timing* of that day, Jesus seemed much more interested in the disciples' *readiness* for it. Through several illustrations and parables, Jesus helped his disciples understand what readiness for that day looks like and the end result of that readiness, as well as what is ahead for those who live as if that day is not coming and instead live only for today.

I imagine that if a group of women from our time gathered around Jesus and asked him when he is going to return, he would say the same thing to them that he said to his disciples. In fact, because his inspired Word *is* what he says to us today, we can work our way through the illustrations and parables Jesus told his disciples in his day, recorded in Matthew 24 and 25, to discover how our ministry among women today can help to prepare women for that day. We pick up Jesus's response to his disciples in Matthew 24:37–42:

> For as were the days of Noah, so will be the coming of the Son of Man. For as in those days before the flood they were eating and drinking, marrying and giving in marriage, until the day when Noah entered the ark, and they were unaware until the

flood came and swept them all away, so will be the coming of the Son of Man. Then two men will be in the field; one will be taken and one left. Two women will be grinding at the mill; one will be taken and one left. Therefore, stay awake, for you do not know on what day your Lord is coming.

So the first thing we hear Jesus saying about that day is that *the day of his coming will be a day of judgment. On that day, some will be swept away, while some will be saved.*

When water began to fall from the sky and gush from the earth in Noah's day, people were busy with ordinary life. They were not expecting the judgment that began to fall in the form of raindrops. They were like so many of us women today, so busy with ordinary life—figuring out what plans to make for dinner, or tomorrow's schedule, or the kids' activities, or the big project at work—assuming that life will just keep going on as is, as the days come and go, sensing no threat of the coming judgment. Evidently the very idea of God breaking into human history to judge the evil of humanity, even in Noah's day, was not believable to people—certainly not urgent to them.

And isn't that the case today? Let's face it. The message of the Bible that there is a day coming when all of those who have refused to come into the ark of safety in the person of Jesus Christ will be swept away in a storm of God's judgment, while those who have hidden themselves in Christ will be saved, is easily ridiculed, sidelined, and ignored. It certainly doesn't seem urgent to many women we interact with in an average day.

And it can seem to us that there are more urgent matters to cover in our ministry among women or, at least, more interesting topics. Women desperately need the Bible's perspective to know what is urgent and what simply will not matter into eternity. We all need to be brought to the place where we recognize our need to be saved from a very real coming judgment. We all need to be pointed toward the open arms of Christ, where we can find refuge from this certain judgment through faith in our Savior who died, suffering God's wrath on our behalf, and who rose from the dead, conquering death and sin forever. We all need the gospel.

In his next story (Matt. 24:45–51), Jesus reveals that *the day of his coming will be a day of examination. On that day some will be evicted, while some will be entrusted.*

Jesus speaks of a wise servant who serves the fellow servants in his master's household with faithfulness, contrasting him with a wicked servant who, when his master is delayed, abuses his fellow servants and his master's resources. Upon the master's return, while the wise servant is blessed by being put in charge of all of the master's possessions, the wicked servant is evicted from the master's house and sent to a place of ongoing sorrow and agonizing regret.

Surely this has something to say not specifically to the secular world but to those who have joined themselves to the church, the household of faith: both the figures in this story are servants in the master's house, awaiting his return. This text challenges all those who have heard the call to serve the Master, Jesus, by serving fellow servants in his household of faith. This includes all of us in the church, whether we have leadership responsibilities or are entrusted to care for fellow servants in more unofficial ways, perhaps serving the Master by serving aging parents or growing children or needy neighbors. Are we faithful day by day to "give them their food at the proper time" (v. 45), wisely setting before them not just physical sustenance but the food that will nourish their souls? The day will come when our Master will return and will examine how the ones given responsibility in his household have served him. He will examine our service, looking for the wise and faithful perseverance that reveals hearts transformed by gospel grace.

What promise this story holds out to the woman who seeks to serve the Master in persevering faithfulness and godly wisdom—

that her service matters, that on the day Christ returns, he will give her even greater opportunities for serving him in meaningful ways into eternity. As women today regularly look for ways to contribute significant good works for the betterment of a needy world, we all need to hear, again and again, that good works are significant—not just to make a difference in the world, and not as contributing in any way to our justification, but as loving and eternally valuable service to our Master, who has made a place for us in his house forever. Service to God starts in his house and reaches to eternity. And just think what it will mean to serve him in that day when the futility and frustration of our work, at which we now labor in a world under a curse, will be gone for good.[1]

As we move into chapter 25 of Matthew, Jesus tells two parables that provide further illumination for his disciples, and for us, in regard to what the day of his coming will be like. In the first parable (vv. 1–12) he says that day will be like a wedding day in which ten bridesmaids charged with lighting the way for the wedding party wait for the arrival of the bridegroom. They go out to meet him carrying their oil lamps to usher him and his bride into the wedding feast, but when the bridegroom doesn't come as quickly as they thought he would, the bridesmaids go to sleep. Five of the ten simply are not prepared for such a long time of waiting—they have not brought with them enough oil to keep their lamps burning. So when the bridegroom finally arrives, those five foolish bridesmaids are not prepared to enter into the wedding feast. They want to presume upon the preparedness of the other five to share some of their oil with them. But others' preparedness cannot be presumed upon. And so the foolish bridesmaids are shut out.

Through this story Jesus tells us that *the day of his coming will be a day of feasting. On that day, some will be shut out while some will be welcomed in.*

We simply can't count on sharing the preparedness of other

Christians on that day. Though Christ's people are indeed one body, each member of that body is called to individual faith in him—faith that shows itself in preparing for his return. We can't presume upon the kindness of Christ to let us into the marriage supper of the Lamb at the last minute when he comes if we are not willing to prepare ourselves for his coming now. Being invited to the wedding and asked to participate in it does not assure entrance to it if we are not among the wise who prepare for it.

How many women are sitting in our church gatherings presuming upon the preparedness of those around them or those related to them, or presuming upon the kindness of the bridegroom? No other person, no earthly bridegroom, no heritage of faith or faithful participation among the faithful, can replace an individual relationship with our heavenly bridegroom. Who among our gatherings faces hearing Jesus say to them on that day, "I do not know you"? How we need to hear the warning in this parable from our Bridegroom and be prepared to wait for his arrival, which may take longer than we think. How we need to seek to know him and be known by him—now, as we come to faith in our Savior, and all along the way to meeting him face-to-face on that day. What a meaningful ministry it is—a ministry that will matter forever—to prepare women to meet Christ so that on that day they will be welcomed in instead of shut out of the great feast.

How do we prepare women to meet Christ? We boldly call them to come to Christ rather than assume they have already taken hold of him by faith. We teach them to pay full attention to "the prophetic word . . . as to a lamp shining in a dark place, until the day dawns" (2 Pet. 1:19). We challenge them "to believe the love that God has for us" and abide in that love "so that we may have confidence for the day of judgment" (1 John 4:16–17). We "exhort one another every day, as long as it is called 'today,' that none of you may be hardened by the deceitfulness of sin. For we have come to share in Christ, if indeed we hold our original confidence firm to the end" (Heb. 3:13–14). With "our hope set on the living God," empowered by the Spirit of the risen Christ, we seek to create a culture of vigorous training for godliness among believers, knowing that "godliness is of value in every way, as it holds promise for the present life and also for the life to come" (1 Tim. 4:8, 10).

In the next parable (Matt. 25:14–30), commonly called the "parable of the talents," Jesus reveals that *the day of his coming will be a day of accountability. On that day some will be exposed as slothful, while some will be praised as faithful.*

In this parable the master is leaving on a journey. Before his departure he entrusts various servants with varying amounts of resources. And there is only one expectation: that those resources will be invested for a return for his kingdom. The servants who receive the five talents and the two talents go "at once" and trade profitably so that what was entrusted to them doubles in value for the master's estate. But the servant entrusted with one talent "dug in the ground and hid his master's money" (v. 18). And then "after a long time" the master returns. Upon his arrival, he settles accounts (v. 19).

In this parable, each of the servants is called to give account— those who have been good stewards of the master's resources as well as those who have not. The truth about their stewardship becomes clear to all in that day of accountability. In various places throughout the Scriptures we are told that this is exactly what will happen on the day when Christ returns. When Jesus comes, he will settle accounts with his servants. "For we must *all* appear before the judgment seat of Christ," Paul wrote to the believers in Corinth (2 Cor. 5:10). All. Believers and unbelievers.

In his commentary on the book of Matthew, Douglas Sean O'Donnell says that the coming judgment is the most neglected theme in the church. He continues: "The second most neglected theme is the theme that the church shall be judged: 'judgment [will]

. . . begin [with] the household of God' (1 Pet. 4:17). The third most neglected theme is the theme that the individual Christian shall stand before the Judgment Seat of Christ to give an account for what he has done (Matt. 16:27; cf. Rom. 14:12)."[2]

I suppose the big question we must all face in light of this coming accountability is this: Am I vulnerable? When I give an account, will it result in being exposed as slothful or praised as faithful? Will I be ejected or rewarded? As we consider this question, and as we consider the implications of this day of accountability for ministry among women, we know this: "There is therefore now no condemnation for those who are in Christ Jesus" (Rom. 8:1). Those who are joined to Christ are as indestructible as Christ. For genuine believers, it will not be their lives that are vulnerable on this day but, rather, their reward. We have trouble understanding completely the nature of such rewards, from the perspective of this earthly life, but we do well to listen to Scripture's references to them. In 1 Corinthians 3:13–15, Paul describes that day of accountability: "The fire will test what sort of work each one has done. If the work that anyone has built on the foundation survives, he will receive a reward. If anyone's work is burned up, he will suffer loss, though he himself will be saved, but only as through fire." It seems that the result of this judgment will be the gain or loss of eternal rewards.

Now you may be thinking, *If Christ paid the price for sin, and if I've confessed my sin and been forgiven, then how can I be held accountable for what I have or haven't done? Isn't it all about what Christ has done?* We cannot confuse God's gift of salvation with his promise of reward. As Randy Alcorn has said, "Salvation is about God's work for us. It's a free gift of grace to which we contribute nothing. Rewards are about our work for God,"[3] which we are equipped and enabled to accomplish by his grace in us.

So what is it that our Master will reward with his praise at his coming? We as women know what gets rewarded in the world, in our society. I can't help but think about the things we as women tend to reward with attention and admiration and compliments. We are so quick to tell each other, "You look so cute!" We admire fashion sense and decorating skill and parenting prowess and academic degrees and increasing income and up-front abilities and even social good. Of course, none of these things is bad in itself, but seeking the temporary reward of the world's approval can distract us from seeking the eternal reward of the Lord's approval.

So what does this parable reveal about what God rewards with his praise? He rewards stewardship, which is simply making the most of what he has entrusted to us in order to increase his estate. He has entrusted each of us as his servants with differing skills, aptitudes, abilities, and opportunities. He has planted us in different places, surrounded by different needs, with differing personalities. We should be asking ourselves: What has God uniquely entrusted to me that I could be investing for a return for his kingdom? What have I buried that I should be investing for the gospel's sake? How has he made me uniquely to expand his kingdom in the world? How can I be a part of developing a culture among women that encourages and praises working for rewards that will last forever? And we should be encouraging each other, affirming the stewardship we see in the lives of others—the way they invest their time in the cause of Christ, the way they develop their talents (and even their bank accounts) to contribute to gospel proclamation, the way they open up their homes to minister the love of Christ, the way they use their stories to tell the story of Christ their redeemer.

On the day of accounting, when we stand before the judgment seat of Christ, we will be called to give an account of how we have invested all that has been entrusted to us. Those women who are mothers will give an account of how they have mothered the children entrusted to them so that there might be an increase in the Master's kingdom. Those of us who have been entrusted with education and opportunity will be held accountable for how we've invested those privileges in ways that extend God's kingdom. Those who have been entrusted with leadership will give an account for how they have led. And because we know that "he who began a good work in you will bring it to completion at the day of Jesus Christ" (Phil. 1:6), we can confidently anticipate hearing our Master say on that day, "Well done, good and faithful servant. You have been faithful over a little; I will set you over much. Enter into the joy of your master" (Matt. 25:21).

What an incredible hope to set before women to take hold of—that as they are joined to Christ by faith, and as his Spirit works in them to produce righteousness, they can anticipate a day when they will not be ashamed but will hear the Master they love say to them, "Well done. Way to go. I entrusted certain things to you—different things than I entrusted to those around you—and you have proved to be a good steward. And because you have been faithful over what I entrusted to you in this life, there is far more I am entrusting to you in the life to come as you now make your home with me and all of those who love me in the new creation. The doors of my home are open to you, and in my home you will experience my joy with me forever."

Our often hard or sorrowful service to our Master during this life looks different when we see it in the light of what is most certainly coming. This "little while," as Peter puts it (1 Pet. 1:6; 5:10), desperately needs the light of eternity for us not only to bear it but to rejoice in it as preparation for living in God's house forever and for calling others to enter this house while it is still today. How important to encourage women to look forward to living in God's house with new and perfect resurrection bodies as we struggle with not just common human ailments but all the unique pains of women's bodies as God has created them, and as they suffer the effects of the fall. How amazing to consider all tears being wiped away, in the midst of many tears. How strengthening to look forward as God's people to a heavenly bridegroom, when so many women struggle with issues relating to earthly ones. All these struggles are also given to us as the Lord's servants to invest and from which we can pray to see increase for his kingdom.

If we are in Christ, this day of accounting is a day not to dread but to joyfully prepare for. We don't need to fear that we haven't done enough. (Don't we, as women, regularly tend to think we haven't done enough or that we simply *aren't* enough?) The real danger being drawn for us in this parable is not the danger of not doing enough for the Master. The two faithful servants receive different amounts and come up with different amounts in the end, and they are both rewarded with exactly the same praise from the Master. The real danger threatens those who do *nothing* with what has been entrusted to them, those for whom there is zero return—no response of faith to the gospel, no treasuring the Master, no fruit of the Spirit, no return for the Master's kingdom—nothing. That's the point of the third servant, who did nothing with his gift. Because he did nothing, he did not just lose his reward; he lost his life.

In the final section of Matthew 25 (vv. 31–46), Jesus speaks of that day as a day of great glory when he will come as king and take his throne. Notice that Jesus is not telling a parable in which we're supposed to figure out that he is the king portrayed in the story. He's saying straight out that on that day he will come as king.

> When the Son of Man comes in his glory, and all the angels with him, then he will sit on his glorious throne. Before him will be gathered all the nations, and he will separate people one from another as a shepherd separates the sheep from the goats. (Matt. 25:31–32)

In describing the day of his coming, Jesus used an illustration that would have been a very familiar scenario to those listening to him. In those days a shepherd often tended both sheep and goats, and when they were out in the field, the sheep and the goats grazed together. But when it came time for them to come in from the cold, the sheep and the goats had to be separated because they were different. This picture of separating two different species is what Jesus uses to describe the separation of those who belong to him through faith in him from those who do not.

Through this parable, Jesus says that *the day of his coming will be a day of separation. On that day, some will be cursed while some will be blessed.* It is a sobering reality, is it not, that within our churches there may be both sheep and goats? We don't always have the insight to tell the difference. But Jesus does. Ministry among women matters forever because this great day of separation is truly coming. Women's ministry offers a crucial, specific, and personal context in which women can consistently and unashamedly call one another, according to the Word, to "examine yourselves, to see whether you are in the faith" (2 Cor. 13:5).

Jesus says that on that day when he comes he will say to his sheep: "For I was hungry and you gave me food, I was thirsty and you gave me drink, I was a stranger and you welcomed me, I was naked and you clothed me, I was sick and you visited me, I was in prison and you came to me" (Matt. 25:35–36). But the sheep respond by asking Jesus *when* they did these things for him, to which he replies: "Truly, I say to you, as you did it to one of the least of these my brothers, you did it to me" (v. 40).

Notice that Jesus is speaking here of what is done for his brothers. And who are Jesus's brothers? "Whoever does the will of my Father in heaven is my brother and sister and mother," he said (Matt. 12:50). So Jesus is talking specifically about what believers do for their hungry, needy, naked, imprisoned brothers and sisters in Christ. Because believers are members of the body of Christ, what is done for the believer is done for Christ. We see this same way of speaking of Christ's connectedness to believers when we read in Acts that Jesus said to Saul, who had been persecuting Christians, "Saul, Saul, why are you persecuting *me?*" (Acts 9:4). To serve believers is to serve Christ; to persecute believers is to persecute Christ.

As I think about sisters serving "the least of these" in the body of Christ, I think of women who are always the first to step up and serve in the nursery or children's ministry, selflessly serving the "least of these" by changing diapers and serving goldfish crackers and telling Bible stories. I think of a sister in Christ who, week by week, picks up a woman in our church who is confined to a wheelchair to drive her back and forth to Bible study. I think of the team of women with nursing skills who worked out a schedule to spend time daily with another woman facing her last days of life as cancer took its toll. I think of a woman who regularly packs up the best of what has been given to the clothes-closet ministry to send to missionary families. I think of the widow who joyfully invests herself in corresponding with prisoners, going over their Bible study curriculum answers and giving feedback. The day will come when these women will hear Jesus say, "Come, you who are blessed by my Father, inherit the kingdom prepared for you from the foundation of the world" (Matt. 25:34).

Of course, some seek to use this passage to challenge us to get busy in the world feeding the hungry, welcoming strangers, and visiting the sick, if we want to be welcomed in on that day. But Jesus is not saying this is what we must do if we want to be blessed instead of cursed. He's saying these are the things we will be doing if we are truly sheep of his fold. This kind of loving, selfless giving to our brothers and sisters in Christ—especially those suffering and in need and imprisoned for the gospel's sake—will be a natural out-flow of our lives, giving evidence that we are sheep and not goats in the midst of the sheep. He's giving us a way to examine ourselves to see if we are in the faith.

As we minister among women, we should never presume that a woman involved in our church, or a woman who uses spiritual or even "Jesus-y" talk, has come from death to life spiritually. We should be looking for responsiveness to God's Word and love for God's people. We should be looking for the kind of others-centered living that Jesus describes here as that which grows out of a connectedness to him. Consider that as Jesus talked about the sheep and the goats, he was speaking to his disciples. In the next few days, one of those disciples would be exposed as a goat by his betrayal of Jesus. Even among the disciples there was a goat, a goat not recognized by the sheep.

We so often want to rush toward offering assurance of salvation to women who come to us troubled and questioning the genuineness of their conversion. Perhaps wise ministry among women considers the reality of the sheep and the goats and does not move too quickly or automatically toward the assumption of assurance. Perhaps the gripping reality of the eternal life ahead for the sheep, as well as the eternal punishment ahead for the goats, should prompt us consistently to give a gospel call to embrace Christ. When we study the Word together—this Word which makes us "wise for salvation through faith in Christ Jesus" (2 Tim. 3:15)—we will not be able to avoid its insistent and comprehensive gospel message. We must keep speaking the Bible's whole, life-and-death truth to one another, both when we are welcoming women who clearly do not yet know Christ, and even when everyone in the room or reading the blog or sitting around the table of conversation has been around the church for a very long time.

When we consider how hard it is for a woman who thinks of herself as one who knows and is known by Christ to recognize that she has never truly trusted Christ in a saving way—that she has been wrong in her estimation of her spiritual condition—we realize how much we need the Holy Spirit to do what only he can do. Surely this means that much of our ministry among women must be a ministry of prayer. We know that "the wind blows where it wishes, and you hear its sound, but you do not know where it comes from or where it goes. So it is with everyone who is born of the Spirit" (John 3:8). So ministry among women takes us to our knees, as we ask the Holy Spirit to blow through our churches, through our homes, and through the lives of women who face eternal separation apart from the Spirit's saving, enlivening work in them.

In Jesus's illustrations and parables, offered in response to the question of when the day will be when he comes again, we've seen that what matters more than knowing *when* he is coming is being *prepared* for his coming, whenever it may be. The message of persevering and waiting and preparing for his coming continues throughout the New Testament. The apostle Paul told the Corinthians to "wait for the revealing of our Lord Jesus Christ, who will sustain you to the end" (1 Cor. 1:7–8). He prayed for the Thessalonians that "the Lord [will] make you increase and abound in love for one another and for all, as we do for you, so that he may establish your hearts blameless in holiness before our God and Father, at the coming of our Lord Jesus with all his saints" (1 Thess. 3:12–13). The writer of Hebrews told the early Jewish converts to hold on tight to their hope in Christ, to stir up one another to love and good works, and not to neglect meeting together but to encourage one another "all the more as you see the Day drawing near" (Heb. 10:22–25).

My friends, the day is drawing near. That's why ministry among women today will matter forever, because women are facing forever. Each one of us will be:

- forever swept away or forever secure in his presence;
- forever consigned to untold agony or forever blessed with fruitful work;
- forever shut out from the Bridegroom's presence or forever sharing his feast;

- forever cast into the outer darkness or forever enveloped in the Master's joy;
- forever cursed in eternal fire or forever blessed with eternal life.

The work of ministry among women will matter forever because "in the Lord [our] labor is not in vain" (1 Cor. 15:58). Paul's prayer for the Philippians connects our labors of this day to the certain hope of the day of Christ's coming:

It is my prayer that your love may abound more and more, with knowledge and all discernment, so that you may approve what is excellent, and so be pure and blameless for the day of Christ, filled with the fruit of righteousness that comes through Jesus Christ, to the glory and praise of God (Phil. 1:9–11).

Acknowledgments

Many thanks to these women who shared their responses to questions for chapter 9, "Gifts and Giftedness: Finding the Place to Serve."

Pam Brown, volunteer coordinator and small-group coleader, Trinity Bible Church (independent), South Sutton, New Hampshire

Esther Lopez de Ramirez, women's ministry worker, Evangelical Presbyterian Church of Peru, Los Rosales, Cajamarca, Peru

Linda Green, director of women's ministry, The Orchard Evangelical Free Church, Arlington Heights, Illinois

Patricia Henry, pastor's wife and children's ministry leader, Metropolitan Evangelistic Church, Lavender Hill, Cape Town, South Africa

Christine Hoover, pastor's wife, Charlottesville Community Church (Southern Baptist), Charlottesville, Virginia

Kathy Keller, director of communication and senior pastor's wife, Redeemer Presbyterian Church (PCA), New York, New York

Leonie Mason, staff worker with the Associate Scheme training program, St. Helen's Bishopsgate (Anglican), London, UK

Hepzibah Shekhar, women's worker and Sunday school ministry coordinator, Zion Church, Lucknow, Uttar Pradesh, India

Sandra Smith, pastor's wife and women's ministry coordinator, New City Fellowship (PCA), Chattanooga, Tennessee

Leeann Stiles, deacon of women's training, Redeemer Church of Dubai, Dubai, United Arab Emirates

Contributors

Kristie Anyabwile is the wife of a church-planting pastor, mom of three, and a discipler of women. She and her family reside in Southeast Washington, DC. She enjoys speaking and writing about motherhood, marriage, and ministry. She strives, by God's grace, to be a Titus 2 woman in a Romans 1 world.

Cindy Cochrum is the director of the women's Bible study at College Church in Wheaton, Illinois. She teaches women, trains leaders, and has written studies in Mark (*Meeting the King*) and Ruth and Esther (*God's Woman in God's Place in God's Time*; coauthored). Cindy and her husband, Kent, have four children and one daughter-in-law.

Ellen Mary Dykas (MA, Covenant Theological Seminary) serves as the women's ministry coordinator for Harvest USA, a national ministry focused on gospel-centered discipleship and teaching regarding sexuality. She coauthored *Sexual Sanity for Women: Healing from Relational and Sexual Brokenness*, and a mini-booklet, *Sex and the Single Girl: Smart Ways to Care for Your Heart*.

Keri Folmar (JD, Loyola Law School, Los Angeles), wife of John, senior pastor of the United Christian Church of Dubai, and mother of three teenagers, writes, teaches, and leads women's Bible studies at her church. She has authored *Joy! A Bible Study on Philippians for Women; Faith* (on James); and *Grace* (on Ephesians).

Gloria Furman (MACE, Dallas Theological Seminary) serves as a cross-cultural worker in the United Arab Emirates where her husband, Dave, pastors Redeemer Church of Dubai. She is the mother of four children and the author of *Glimpses of Grace*; *Treasuring Christ When Your Hands Are Full*; and *The Pastor's Wife*.

Nancy Guthrie teaches the Bible through numerous Bible study books; at her home church, Cornerstone Presbyterian Church in Franklin, Tennessee; and at conferences nationally and internationally. She offers companionship and biblical insight to the grieving through books, through retreats for bereaved parents, and through the GriefShare video series presented with her husband, David.

Susan Hunt has been married to retired pastor Gene Hunt for fifty years. They have three children and twelve grandchildren. She is the former director of women's ministry for the Presbyterian Church in America and has written several books for women, including *Spiritual Mothering: The Titus 2 Model for Women Mentoring Women*.

Kathleen Nielson (PhD, Vanderbilt University) is director of women's initiatives for The Gospel Coalition. She has taught English, directed women's Bible studies at several churches, and speaks and writes extensively. Kathleen and Niel live in Wheaton, Illinois, and have three sons, two daughters-in-law, and four granddaughters.

Carrie Sandom (BTh, University of Oxford) has been involved in women's ministry for over twenty years and is based at St. John's, Tunbridge Wells, where she works with women of all ages and stages of life. A regular conference speaker, Carrie is also the director of the Women's Ministry Stream at the Cornhill Training Course in London.

Claire Smith (PhD, Moore Theological College/University of Western Sydney) has a Bible-teaching ministry among women in Sydney (where she and her husband, Rob, make their home), throughout Australia, and internationally. Along with her published doctorate examining "teaching" in 1 Corinthians, 1 and 2 Timothy, and Titus, she also wrote *God's Good Design: What the Bible Really Says about Men and Women.*

$\mathcal{N}otes$

Chapter 1: The Word at the Center

1. John M. Frame, *The Doctrine of the Word of God* (Phillipsburg, NJ: P&R, 2010), 3.

Chapter 2: The Word on Women

1. http://www.smh.com.au/national/girls-boys-and-toys-call-to-end-stereotyping -20131106-2x21m.html, accessed January 3, 2014.
2. See http://www.playunlimited.org.au/2013/11/27/dolls-trucks-workplace -gender-divide/, accessed January 3, 2014.
3. http://www.mercurynews.com/business/ci_25134482/here-are-facebooks-56 -gender-identity-options, accessed April 10, 2014.
4. This is not to deny that some people have ambiguous physiological gender, and certainly not to deny they are fully made in the image of God, equally loved by him. These rare disorders, like all frailty and suffering, are tragic evidence of the disruption and distortion our human rebellion from God caused in his good creation; they are not part of God's original intention for humanity (cf. Rom. 8:19–22). We can praise God that these days more resources and research are going toward helping people with these disorders.
5. God is like a mother hen (Matt. 23:37) and a nurse (Num. 11:12). He gives birth to his people (Deut. 32:18; James 1:18) and cares like a mother (Ps. 131; Isa. 66:13).
6. For instance, by only ever addressing God as "God" and never as "Father." More radically, others attempt to address God as "Mother" or "Goddess."
7. Paul implies woman is made in the image of God when he leaves out the "image" statement in the last phrase of verse 7. Paul knows that God created man in his image, male and female. His interest here is in the difference between men and women in terms of glory.
8. While we are personally either sons or daughters of God, God's children (Rom. 8:16–17), we are also all—male and female—"*sons* of God," because our filial relationship with the Father is established in the Son, and through him we receive the Spirit of the Son and the privileges and inheritance of a "son" (Gal. 4:1–7).
9. Heb. *ishshah*, "woman"; *ish*, "man."

10. Most Bible translations follow the convention explained in the ESV footnote for Ex. 3:15: "The word LORD, when spelled with capital letters, stands for the divine name, 'YHWH,' in the original Hebrew text."
11. Deut. 33:29; Pss. 33:20; 70:5; 115:9, 10, 11.
12. Isa. 30:5; Ezek. 12:14; Hos. 13:9.
13. See Rev. 12:9; 20:2; 2 Cor. 11:3–4, cf. 2:11; 11:14, and also Luke 10:18–20.
14. Rom. 6:3–11; 8:29; 1 Cor. 15:49; 2 Cor. 3:18; Col. 3:10.
15. See Wayne Grudem, "The Meaning of *kephalê* ('Head'): An evaluation of New Evidence, Real and Alleged," *Biblical Foundations for Manhood and Womanhood* (Wheaton, IL: Crossway, 2002), 145–202, repr. from *JETS* 44/1 (March 2001): 25–65; *Evangelical Feminism and Biblical Truth* (Colorado Springs, CO: Multnomah, 2004), 201–11, 552–99.
16. Although many are still enslaved by other means such as child labor, prostitution, people trafficking, sex slavery, and other types of exploitation and loss of freedom.
17. 1 Cor. 7:21; Eph. 6:5–9; Col. 3:22–4:1; 1 Tim. 6:1–2; Philem. 10–16; 1 Pet. 2:18–21.
18. See, e.g., Denny Burk, *What Is the Meaning of Sex?* (Wheaton, IL: Crossway, 2013); Claire Smith, *God's Good Design: What the Bible Really Says about Men and Women* (Sydney, AU: Matthias Media, 2012).
19. E.g., Rom. 12:3–8; 1 Cor. 12:4–30; Eph. 4:11.
20. E.g., 1 Cor. 3:5–10; 16:15–16; Eph. 4:12; Phil. 1:1; 1 Thess. 5:12; 1 Tim. 3:1–13; 5:18; Heb. 13:7; 1 Pet. 5:1.
21. E.g., Gal. 6:6; 1 Tim. 3:6.
22. E.g., 1 Cor. 7:17–35; 2 Cor. 12–15; Phil. 2:25–30; 1 Tim. 5:13; 6:17–18.
23. E.g., 1 Cor. 12:22–26; 14:5–6, 9–19, 23–24, 26–39.
24. E.g., 1 Tim. 5:1–14; Titus 2:2–6; 1 Pet. 5:5.
25. See the discussion of this text by Mark Thompson, "The Theological Ground of Evangelical Complementarianism," in *Women, Sermons and the Bible* (Sydney, AU: Matthias Media, 2014).
26. 1 Tim. 2:7; 3:2; 4:11, 13; 6:2; 2 Tim. 1:11; 2:2, 24; 3:10, 16; 4:2.
27. E.g., 1 Tim. 3:1–7; 4:11–16; 2 Tim. 2:24–25.
28. Acts 16:13–15; 17:4, 12.
29. Acts 12:12; 16:40; Rom. 16:3–5; 1 Cor. 16:19; Col. 4:15.
30. Acts 1:14; 21:5, 9; 1 Cor. 11:5; 1 Tim. 5:5.
31. Acts 18:2; Rom. 16:4; Phil. 4:2–3.
32. Acts 8:3; 22:4; Rom. 16:6, 7, 17; 1 Cor. 9:5.
33. Rom. 16:16; 2 Tim. 4:21; Philem. 2.
34. E.g., Acts 2:42–47; 1 Cor. 2:7; 11:26; 14:25; 2 Cor. 10:7 (NRSV); 1 Thess. 1:3, 7; 5:11.
35. The word *gunaikas* in the original language can mean "women" or "wives." In this context, following on from 3:8, it could be translated: "Likewise, women [deacons] must . . . ," or, "Likewise, the wives [of deacons] must . . ." The ESV prefers the latter.
36. E.g., 1 Cor. 14:26, 31; 1 Thess. 5:11.

Chapter 3: The Word Passed On

1. This is not meant in any way to undermine the role of the elders or imply that other ministries carry the same authority; they clearly do not (see chap. 2). The elders, as they "pass it on" in their authoritative roles, both model and oversee the process of "passing it on" as it occurs within many segments of a congregation.

2. Paul says something similar in 1 Tim. 6:11–12 and 2 Tim. 1:13–14.

3. See, e.g., 1 Tim. 3:1.

4. The other passage is 1 Tim. 3:1–7. The criteria for appointing deacons are outlined in 1 Tim. 3:8–13, but as the role of deacon was not a formal teaching role, they are not expected to teach (although the other criteria are much the same).

5. See 1 Tim. 3:4–5.

6. See 1 Tim. 3:6.

7. See 2 Tim. 1:5.

8. Elsewhere, of course, Paul urges Timothy not to let people look down on his youth, indicating that spiritual maturity can be found among those who are younger than the people they seek to serve (see 1 Tim. 4:12).

9. See, e.g., Titus 1:12–13.

10. Paul affirms this in Titus 2:11–14.

11. See 2 Tim. 3:6.

12. When Jesus addressed the rich young ruler, he said that only God is good; see Mark 10:18 or Luke 18:19.

13. See Titus 1:12.

14. The noble wife of Proverbs 31 had many roles outside the home, but it's clear that her husband and children remained her central focus.

15. See Eph. 5:22 and Col. 3:18.

16. The writer to the Hebrews says much the same thing in Heb. 12:7–11.

17. See Rom. 3:25 and 8:1 where Paul makes this clear.

18. See, e.g., Carrie Sandom, "Equipped for Every Good Work: Profitable Handling of the Scriptures," address, The Gospel Coalition 2012 National Women's Conference, http://resources.thegospelcoalition.org/library/equipped-for-every-good-work-profitable-handling-of-the-scriptures-2-timothy-3-17. It includes some of the tools needed for understanding the New Testament Epistles. See also Carrie Sandom, "Bible Toolkit #2: Rightly Handling the Word of Truth," which presents the tools needed for unpacking Old Testament narrative. http://resources.thegospelcoalition.org/library/bible-toolkit-2-rightly-handling-the-word-of-truth.

19. *Two Ways to Live* is a seven-session training course by Phillip Jensen and Tony Payne, rev. ed. (Sydney, AU: Matthias Media, 1998), that comes with a leader's manual and a workbook for group members. A downloadable app is available as well.

20. I have led groups through courses offered by The Good Book College (www.thegoodbookcollege.co.uk), which is based on the Moore College Correspondence Course (www.moore.edu.au/distance). Other good, solidly biblical distance-learning opportunities are available.

21. More information on the Cornhill Training Course is available from the Proclamation Trust website, www.proctrust.org.uk/cornhill.

22. The annual Proclamation Trust Women in Ministry Conference provides a network for women in Bible teaching ministry in the UK as well as opportunities for honing their Bible teaching skills; www.proctrust.org.uk/conferences. The Charles Simeon Trust, based in Chicago, runs similar workshops in the US; www.simeontrust.org.

Chapter 4: The Local Church

1. Nayana's name has been changed.

2. John Stott, *Basic Christian Leadership* (Downers Grove, IL: InterVarsity, 2002), 17.

3. Charles Hodge, *1 Corinthians* (Wheaton, IL: Crossway, 1995), 219.

4. Ron Bentz, *The Unfinished Church: God's Broken and Redeemed Work-in-Progress* (Wheaton, IL: Crossway, 2014), 37.

Chapter 5: The World around Us

1. Thomas Chalmers, "The Expulsive Power of a New Affection," sermon (1817), http://manna.mycpanel.princeton.edu/rubberdoc/c8618ef3f4a7b542 4f710c5fb61ef281.pdf.

2. Gen. 17:3; Judg. 6:22; 13:22; Isa. 6:5; Ezek. 1:28; 3:23; 43:3; 44:4; Dan. 8:17; Mark 9:6; Acts 9:4; Rev. 1:17.

3. "Chicago Statement on Biblical Inerrancy" (Chicago: International Council on Biblical Inerrancy, 1978). A published copy of the statement may be found in Carl F. H. Henry, *God, Revelation, and Authority*, vol. 4 (Waco, TX: Word, 1979), 211–19.

Chapter 7: Older and Younger

1. Westminster Larger Catechism (Atlanta: Presbyterian Church in America Committee for Christian Education & Publications, 1990), 4.

2. "The covenant of grace is the sovereignly initiated arrangement by which the Triune God lives in saving favor and merciful relationship with His people. Because we are in union with Him, we are united to His other children. So the covenant of grace defines our relationship to God and to one another. It orders a way of life that flows out of a promise of life. To realize this is to think and live covenantally." J. Ligon Duncan and Susan Hunt, *Women's Ministry in the Local Church* (Wheaton, IL: Crossway, 2006), 32.

3. Westminster Confession of Faith, chap. 26, "Of the Communion of Saints" (Atlanta: Presbyterian Church in America Committee for Christian Education & Publications, 1990), 85.

4. Susan Hunt, *Spiritual Mothering* (Wheaton, IL: Crossway, 1992), 12.

5. See *Women's Ministry in the Local Church*, Appendix 2. An expanded version, as well as a section on training T2D leaders, is in the *Women's Ministry Training and Resource Guide*, a publication of the Committee on Discipleship Ministries of the Presbyterian Church in America, http://www.cepbookstore.com.

6. TRUE, a three-year curriculum for teen girls, is also published by the Committee on Discipleship Ministries of the Presbyterian Church in America, http://www.mytrueteen.com. It can be adapted for elementary-age girls. Other resources: Susan Hunt and Mary A. Kassian, *Becoming God's True Woman: While I Still Have a Curfew*, new ed. (Chicago: Moody, 2012); and Susan Hunt and Richie Hunt, *Cassie and Caleb Discover God's Wonderful Design*, new ed. (Chicago: Moody, 2013).

7. Matthew Henry, *Matthew Henry's Concise Commentary on the Whole Bible*, "John 13:34–35" (accessed 12/15/2014), *Bible Hub: Online Bible Study Suite*, http://biblehub.com/commentaries/mhc/john/13.htm).

Chapter 8: Sexual Wholeness

1. Details changed for confidentiality.

2. These issues are addressed more fully in the Harvest USA women's discipleship curriculum, *Sexual Sanity for Women: Healing from Relational and Sexual Brokenness*, ed. Ellen Dykas (Greensboro, NC: New Growth Press, 2013).

3. Similar to a married couple's commitment not to allow any third-party influences into their sexual intimacy, such a commitment for singles would prohibit engagement in any form of sexual activity with anyone *or anything*: a friend, self, objects—either directly or through the use of technology, i.e., sexting, phone sex, online sexual chat rooms.

4. John 14:23 is the beautiful promise Jesus gave to come and make a home in his disciples. He described this idea of home powerfully through the teaching in John 15, in which he proclaims himself as the true vine and his followers as the branches who abide (make a home) in him.

5. I've found in my own ministry of Bible teaching and discipleship that women respond eagerly when issues pertaining to sexuality are woven in as a normal part of the curriculum. In fact, many women are grateful to have sexual matters brought up because they don't know how to talk about it. We need to help Christian women gain a biblical theology of these matters and vocabulary to know how to engage the conversation.

6. I'm indebted to Dr. Paul Tripp, former faculty member at the Christian Counseling and Educational Foundation, who used this term in lectures for his 2006 class, *Methods of Biblical Change*.

7. There is wisdom in encouraging women to have more than one accountability partner and helper as it diffuses any temptation toward unhealthy dependence.

8. Accountability and a commitment to live in the light will be both inconvenient and costly but supremely worth it!

Chapter 9: Gifts and Giftedness

1. Respondents are listed in the acknowledgments.

2. Complementarians in different cultures tend to use the term *preach* in diverse ways. Americans most often would *not* say that women preach (meaning that women are not ordained to offer authoritative teaching in the gathered worship of God's people). Those in the United Kingdom and Australia, for

example, often seem quite comfortable referring to women preaching (as in expounding the Word of God to one another).

Chapter 10: Ultimate Goals

1. Rom. 8:18–25.
2. Douglas Sean O'Donnell, *Matthew: All Authority in Heaven and on Earth* (Wheaton, IL: Crossway, 2013), 725.
3. Randy Alcorn, "Questions to Randy Alcorn about Eternal Rewards," March 2, 2010, http://www.epm.org/resources/2010/Mar/2/questions-randy-alcorn -about-eternal-rewards/.

General Index

Scripture Index

l

THE GOSPEL COALITION

The Gospel Coalition is a fellowship of evangelical churches deeply committed to renewing our faith in the gospel of Christ and to reforming our ministry practices to conform fully to the Scriptures. We have committed ourselves to invigorating churches with new hope and compelling joy based on the promises received by grace alone through faith alone in Christ alone.

We desire to champion the gospel with clarity, compassion, courage, and joy—gladly linking hearts with fellow believers across denominational, ethnic, and class lines. We yearn to work with all who, in addition to embracing our confession and theological vision for ministry, seek the lordship of Christ over the whole of life with unabashed hope in the power of the Holy Spirit to transform individuals, communities, and cultures.

Through its women's initiatives, The Gospel Coalition aims to support the growth of women in faithfully studying and sharing the Scriptures; in actively loving and serving the church; and in spreading the gospel of Jesus Christ in all their callings.

Join the cause and visit TGC.org for fresh resources that will equip you to love God with all your heart, soul, mind, and strength, and to love your neighbor as yourself.

TGC.org

Also Available from **Crossway and The Gospel Coalition**